"Real change is real hard and takes real time. But it can be done — it's just that it can't be done easily. Doyle and Pimentel show, step by step, how to translate the education reform rhetoric into practical local reality. Teachers will welcome this thoughtful and real-to-life action guide."

— Adam Urbanski, president, Rochester, NY,
Teachers Association, and vice president,
American Federation of Teachers

"*Raising the Standard* is a clear, practical and concise guide for school improvement. Parents, educators and community leaders will find it extremely valuable."

— Diane Ravitch, senior fellow, Brookings Institution, and
former U.S. assistant secretary of education

"Two of America's preeminent educators, Denis P. Doyle and Susan Pimentel, have created an extraordinary toolkit that empowers communities to create enduring and meaningful school improvements. *Raising the Standard* is written simply, powerfully, and directly. It carefully guides communities to get the job done."

— Sonia Hernandez, deputy superintendent,
California Department of Education

"*Raising the Standard* moves the standards debate from theory to practice. Based on hard-won experience in schools across the country, it is tough-minded, practical and inspirational. And its emphasis on local control is unique, laying out a blueprint for change that any school district in America can adopt and adapt."

— David T. Kearns, former Xerox chairman and CEO, and
former U.S. deputy secretary of education

"This book is 'must reading' for teachers, principals, central office administrators, superintendents, school board members, or anyone else helping school districts to become standards-based. I wish it had been available when we began our standards work in Chicago."

— Patricia A. Harvey, senior fellow,
National Center on Education and the Economy,
and former chief accountability officer, Chicago Public Schools

# RAISING THE STANDARD

Denis P. Doyle, Susan Pimentel

An eight-step
action guide
for schools and
communities

CORWIN PRESS, INC.
A Sage Publications Company
Thousand Oaks, California

*For information:*

Corwin Press, Inc.
A Sage Publications Company
2455 Teller Road
Thousand Oaks, California 91320

SAGE Publications Ltd.
6 Bonhill Street
London EC2A 4PU
United Kingdom

SAGE Publications India Pvt. Ltd.
M-32 Market
Greater Kailash I
New Delhi 110 048 India

Printed in the United States of America

**Library of Congress Cataloging-in-Publication Data**

Doyle, Denis P.
    Raising the standard: An eight-step action guide for schools and communities/Denis P. Doyle and Susan Pimentel.
        p.  cm.
    Includes index.
    ISBN 0-8039-6707-1 (pbk.: acid-free paper. — ISBN 0-8039-6706-3 (cloth: acid-free paper)
    1. School improvement programs — United States — Case studies.
2. Education — Standards — United States — Case studies. 3. Educational change — United States — Case studies. 4. Community and school — United States — Case studies.  I. Pimentel, Susan. II. Title.
LB2822.82.D69    1997
        371.2′07′0973—dc21                                    97-33893

This book is printed on acid-free paper.

97 98 99 00 01 02 03 10 9 8 7 6 5 4 3 2 1

Project Management and Design: KSA Group, Inc.
Illustration: Tom Smith

# TABLE OF CONTENTS

## AN *EDUCATION REFORM* MÖBIUS STRIP: METAPHOR FOR REFORM

A Möbius strip (invented by German mathematician August Möbius in 1868) is described by Webster as "a one-sided surface that is constructed from a rectangle by holding one end fixed, rotating the opposite end through 180° and applying it to the first end." A Möbius strip is the graphic element that weaves throughout this book to provide you a reform talisman.

Enclosed in this book is an *Education Reform* Möbius strip. Twist it 180° and tape it to itself. Then draw a continuous line down the middle. What began as a flat piece of paper now looks like a three-dimensional helix, *and the pencil line becomes continuous, circling back and connecting with itself.* Like successful school reform, there is no beginning, no end, no middle, no finish line. Applying the right torque to a structure — a flat slip of paper or a school district — produces depth and complexity. The paper is transformed, just as this eight-step process can transform schools.

To complete the metaphor, hold the *Education Reform* Möbius strip at an incline and look at the line you've drawn. Not only does it have no beginning and no end, but as it winds it also steadily climbs upward.

You can begin with Step 1 or enter the process at any step and work up, down and through the remaining steps. To complete Step 8, return to Step 1. ...

## ABOUT THIS BOOK

This book — written for both the interested layman and professional — describes the process and content of standards-driven education reform. Only the highlights appear in the hard copy of this book; the full text (including hypertext) is contained in an "electronic book," the CD-ROM tucked into the back cover. The full text, as well as many supplementary materials, also is available on *Goal Line*, the education reform online network.

The reason for three types of presentation? The general reader (as well as the professional) needs only an overview of the process we describe; this book should be enough.

## CD-ROM VERSION

The reader who needs more detail, however, will find it in our CD-ROM or online. For example, teachers and students may want to delve into the subject of standards — and full-text examples of other state and district standards — more fully than citizens at large. School business officers need to know more about financial matters than teachers, students or board members find interesting or useful. And so on. Busy readers need a minimal amount of copy to wade through, but they also need to have confidence that additional backup is available. This format permits readers of all levels of interest and sophistication to "drill" into the subject matter, going only as deep as they need to.

In fact, the CD-ROM is an "exploded" version of the hard copy, using hypertext to give the reader easy access to voluminous material, including more explanatory narrative, extensive anecdotes, samples and examples (such as the full text of the **Beaufort County, SC**, and **Colorado**, **Delaware** and **Virginia** standards, as well as the **California English Language Arts standards matrix**). You'll find these hyperlinks indicated in the book like this:

**Beaufort County, SC**    or    ➤ **Beaufort County, SC**

If you click on these links on the CD-ROM, you'll access more information about that topic. The CD-ROM permits us to "interact" with the reader by allowing the reader to interact with the text. It also provides practical symmetry because the reader becomes his or her own publisher, downloading or viewing only what is needed when it's needed (the literary counterpart to "just-in-time delivery," in which producers take from suppliers only what they need, when they need it and deliver only what customers need as they need it).

## ONLINE VERSION

*Goal Line* is an electronic service of the Coalition for Goals 2000. It permits readers to receive regular updates using proprietary software and the Internet and to contribute to *Raising the Standard: An Eight-Step Action Guide for Schools and Communities* as they learn more. All of the beta site districts participate on *Goal Line*, so it's easy to get in touch with the folks in the trenches. In this format, then, this becomes a two-way book, one to which the reader may contribute.

# ACKNOWLEDGMENTS

We must first extend our thanks to all the people who made this book possible: the nation's students and teachers. We owe a special debt of gratitude to Bruce Cooper for his unstinting support and keen editorial eye, as well as to our "teachers": Lamar Alexander, Brad Butler, Lou Gerstner, David Kearns and John Murphy, and others too numerous to mention. Equally important, this effort could not have been brought to a successful conclusion without our primary model, Charlotte-Mecklenburg, NC, which pioneered most of what appears in these pages, and our main beta site, Beaufort County, SC, which helped to field test, modify and improve the Charlotte-Mecklenburg strategies.

The Beaufort work began under the previous superintendent, Dick Flynn, and has continued under the leadership of Herman Gaither. Beaufort is not only a community of exceptional beauty and great diversity, but it also is made up of risk-takers and visionaries, a number of whom were members of Beaufort 2000. Several years ago, Beaufort 2000 began the daunting task of putting education reform on the public agenda. In particular, Bill Marsher, Bonnie Smith and Norm Harberger are to be commended for their hard work and prescience and for seeing the process through from beginning to end. An example of the extraordinary work Beaufort 2000 has done appears in an appendix as an inspiration to other communities across the nation; throughout this report, we spotlight the work of the Beaufort schools.

Like all good stories, there is much good luck in this one: The Beaufort Process, as we have come to think of it, was triggered by former Carnegie Foundation education program officer Alden Dunham's discovery of Charlotte-Mecklenburg's standards. He blithely assumed that if Charlotte could do it, so could Beaufort. He was right, but in ways that no one could have foreseen at the time.

The members of the Beaufort County School Board, chaired by Laura Bush, are to be commended for their boldness and vision. Indeed, each board member has played a special role: Earl Campbell, Rick Caporale, Chip Floyd, Dale Friedman (secretary of the board), Craig Germain (retired), York Glover (immediate past chairman), Reuben Green, Susan Jancourtz, Charles Kresh (vice chairman), Jim Lambright (retired) and Bonnie Smith. It is hard to imagine a more diverse board — five members are black, six white; three are female, eight male — and they represent a full spectrum of the community, geographically and professionally. It is citizen democracy at its best.

We also enjoyed the support and encouragement of an advisory committee who met and conferred with us and read the manuscript in early drafts; their names appear at the back of the book. We must, of course, stress that any weaknesses that remain are the responsibility of the authors.

While this book is a personal statement based on many years of experience working in school districts, we are unusually indebted to several gifted colleagues who have inspired and guided us. Because of Stewart Springfield and the generosity of the Walton Family Foundation, we started and finished this book. A two-year grant from the Foundation in September 1995 provided us the time and opportunity to take what we had learned (both as participants and observers) and commit it to paper.

Many others deserve thanks for their contributions. Leslye A. Arsht, president of the Coalition for Goals 2000, provided constant, enthusiastic encouragement and advice and did much to help bring this book to completion. Her sensitivity to nuance and her discerning eye provided relief during the challenging publication process. Without Rosemary Polanco's and Paul Thallner's (both of the Coalition for Goals 2000) assiduous care and attention to detail, we could not have met our many deadlines. Jay May provided needed clarity and precision in developing the figures for Step 3. Adam Kernan-Schloss, Martha Vockley and Joanne Olson of KSA Group worked with amazing patience to sharpen and organize our ideas and shape up our sometimes esoteric use of language. Tarver Harris of KSA Group gave a brilliant artist's touch to the aesthetic aspects of the book. Tom Smith's Möbius strip is a work of art. Sheree Speakman of Coopers & Lybrand was a perceptive guiding companion during the long drafting phase. We'd also like to thank Alison Auerbach and David Deshryver of Doyle Associates for reading parts of the manuscript and helping to get the appendix into shape.

While the debts to individuals are too numerous to list, we must assume responsibility for the full text and our interpretations of relevant research and site work. Any errors of fact or interpretation are solely our responsibility.

**Denis P. Doyle**  
Chevy Chase, Maryland

**Susan Pimentel**  
Hanover, New Hampshire

# PROLOGUE

## Making the Commitment to World-Class Schools: Community Sketches

*Raising the Standard: An Eight-Step Action Guide for Schools and Communities* lays the groundwork for lasting school reform. Our point of departure is academic standards: setting them and meeting them. Embedded in this process is the conviction that standards matter in education as they do in all other facets of our lives; that standards must have consequences; and that when they are adopted, standards transform schooling. In and of themselves, standards are not a panacea, but they do set the stage for complete reform and restructuring. They are the necessary first step.

- Standards "set" reveal what we expect of our students, schools and communities.

- Standards "met" reveal the extent to which our students, schools and communities meet expectations.

- "Consequences" reveal how seriously we take our responsibilities.

Ignoring these three elements guarantees failure.

<u>*Prisoners of Time*</u>, the 1994 report of the National Education Commission on Time and Learning, advanced a simple but radical idea: The whole edifice of modern schooling is fatally flawed because it emphasizes time rather than mastery. For more than 150 years, American students have received diplomas for spending time in school — regardless of what they have learned.

A standards-based system rationalizes education; students don't graduate until they demonstrate mastery (what they know) and skills (what they can do). Clearly, some students take fewer years to demonstrate mastery than others. Students also master different subjects at different times. But mastery is the only result that counts. It is the bottom line for students — and for schools and districts.

Standards must clearly identify what we expect of students, teachers and schools, and we must see that they are met. Standards are set not to create winners and losers, nor to hold low performers up to ridicule or disgrace, but to create an atmosphere in which students can improve.

Teaching and learning must be the schools' central mission. Performance-driven schools are devices to get your priorities right. Thinking through what you want to accomplish within limits of available money and facilities puts you back in charge.

Genuine, long-lasting reform grows from the grass roots. The more options, the better. That is why, in place of fixed prescription, we advance a new way of thinking that has grown organically out of the American tradition of local control and citizen democracy. This way of thinking weaves together practices that the nation's best schools employ. Based in equal measure on theory — a vision of what modern schooling should do — and hard-won experience gained in the rough-and-tumble world of school district politics, we show you how to restructure schools around learning rather than clocks, calendars and codes. You choose the paths you take to get there; we provide simple, straightforward steps — tried and true — to blaze the trail.

The "lessons learned" that we describe in this short book have been drawn from our experiences in the field, working with ordinary communities that have made an extraordinary commitment to world-class schools. We profile five below, and draw upon them for examples and illustrations throughout the text: **Charlotte-Mecklenburg, NC**; **Beaufort County, SC**; **Guilford, ME**; **Murfreesboro, TN**; and **Red Clay, DE**. These "beta sites" are a microcosm of America, our problems and our opportunities, our challenges and our fears, our limitations and our vision.

Readers should remember that each of the five had a different starting place and each is in a different place on the reform spectrum today. Not one of these districts was so advanced — or is so advanced today — that it is out of reach of other districts. The beta sites began in the real world, and in the real world they remain. Indeed, what distinguishes them and makes them "extraordinary" is their willingness to run risks, not their sophistication. They have no secret weapons or silver bullets. They simply set high standards for themselves.

They also are distinguished by one fact: Each district seized the initiative for reasons of its own. Just as former U.S. Speaker of the House Tip O'Neill knew that "all politics is local," all education reform is local too.

*For Charlotte-Mecklenburg, NC, the nominal catalyst was the business community — which was determined that Charlotte take its place as the jewel in the crown of the "New South" — and the functional catalyst was Superintendent John Murphy. Charlotte is the nation's fourth largest banking center and the hub of a dynamic commercial renewal. But the business community was convinced that to be truly world-class, the city needed world-class schools. As the nation's 29th largest school district, Charlotte had the resources, both human and financial, to do many things smaller districts can only dream about: serious research and development, construction of tests and measures, comprehensive analyses and broadly based professional development. John Murphy's World Class Schools Panel, convened in 1991, was the first step.*

*Thanks to this early start, Charlotte made significant progress and in some respects remains the most advanced of the nation's standards-driven districts.*

*__Beaufort County, SC__, famous because of Pat Conroy's 1990 novel* **The Water Is Wide** *(the story of a one-room school on a remote island), is a study in change. With nearly 15,000 students, Beaufort County barely makes the list of the 500 biggest districts in America. The incentive for change flowed from simple community pride: Old Beaufortonians (both black and white) wanted to reclaim a vaunted past, and newcomers (many vigorous retirees) were convinced that Beaufort schools could be much better. Both groups recognized that a community of Beaufort's vitality would be compromised if its schools were second-rate. Nor could the county compete in regional and national markets. The issue united community leaders from all walks of life, all races and all regions of the 95-island district. What began as a strategic planning exercise quickly became a full-blown standards-setting undertaking that led to new tests, improved professional development and new partnerships with businesses and community groups. It was so successful that* Education Week, *the nation's education paper of record, featured Beaufort as the premier example of a standards-driven district in its special issue on standards. After four years of hard work, Beaufort is using the 1997–98 school year to consolidate gains and will renew its standards-setting initiative in 1998–99. Beaufort has come far, but recognizes that there is no finish line.*

*__Guilford, ME__ is as small and remote as Charlotte is big and central, but the reasons for change were structurally similar: economic development and old-fashioned community pride. Located in the rural Appalachian highlands of western Maine, Guilford is a working-class community with 1,000 students. Its reform effort was led by Norm Higgins, principal of Piscataquis Community High School (the only high school in the county). After serving on Gov. John McKernan's Common Core of Knowledge council in 1990, Higgins became convinced that education was the community's* sine qua non *of economic viability. As a consequence, he became determined to hold his students to world-class standards. Only then would they be able to find and hold satisfying jobs. Among other things, Higgins eliminated "easy" courses and required all students to take a full complement of demanding academic courses to graduate. Now superintendent of the Guilford district, Higgins continues to prove naysayers wrong by refusing to take "no" for an answer. As a result, he is pushing reform down into middle and elementary schools.*

*__Murfreesboro, TN__, Superintendent John Hodge Jones, chairman of the National Education Commission on Time and Learning (which produced* **Prisoners of Time**), *had a vision that schools should serve their communities as they once did, consistent with the realities of modern social and economic life. He was determined to throw out the old academic calendar and replace it with one that both fit the needs of the late 20th century and extended education opportunity* *for the district's 5,500 students. Once the district switched to an extended-day, extended-year format in 1990, the logic of setting up a performance-based system was inexorable. Indeed, the tough question before Murfreesboro is, "Do students learn more in such a system?" The likelihood is high, but the evidence is not yet in. And if the evidence supports the theory, the next questions are "How much more do they learn?" and "Why?"*

*The changes in <u>Red Clay, DE</u>, were driven by the simple conviction that the district's students were not doing well enough academically. School Board President Bill Manning was convinced that the system must have high standards to serve its 14,000 students well; he also was dismayed that the desegregation court order under which the district labored was silent on the issue of academic performance. He believes the purpose of integration is to improve schools, not ignore academics. And he is convinced that when performance improves, community support for schools increases. Among other things, Red Clay is committed to education choice, both to create niches for teachers and students and to stimulate high academic performance. The district is home to Delaware's first charter high school — a science and mathematics school — as well as the state's first charter Montessori school. Red Clay is moving briskly on professional development, community involvement and accountability as well, but has a long road ahead.*

The path to better schools is filled with pitfalls. Goodwill and hard work are not enough. The proponents of systemic change are few, and they are outnumbered by those with a vested interest in the current system, who are ferocious defenders of the *status quo*. Still others wait to see which way the wind blows before committing themselves. They follow success.

Are schools up to the challenge? Schools are parts of bureaucracies, and bureaucracies in any sector are notoriously resistant to change. That's what they are all about: rigid procedures strictly adhered to. Change is threatening to school staffs, just as it is to staffs in most other organizations. But change has an upside: improvement. (The classic definition of "profit" in economics is "reward for taking a risk." This definition holds true for nonprofit organizations as well.) In light of the uncertainty that surrounds change, vigorous organizations go through three steps: They identify the need for change and communicate it to their troops and their customers; they map the change process; and then they implement the change as rapidly as possible. The keys to success are communication and stamina; let people know what the future holds and move aggressively.

While we do not offer a single master template for school reform (there is no such thing), we do offer a process to walk through standards-based school reform from "a" to "z" at the local level, to preserve and reinforce local control while increasing public accountability.

Our approach takes eight steps, and while they appear in linear fashion, many are best executed simultaneously or in quick succession.

The process runs in cycles, moving from involvement to action to assessment and then back again to consensus-building, more action and more assessment. It requires implementing new strategies and tactics on the one hand and, on the other, connecting a critical mass of education's customers to a common vision; the strategy is anchored in the classroom and, at the same time, builds trust among educators, parents and citizens alike.

The eight steps offer a system for transforming schools driven by a coherent vision of higher standards for all students. You can enter the process at any step and work up, down and through the remaining steps. Start where each of the beta sites began by asking:

- Where are we now?

- Where do we want to be?

- How do we get there?

For most schools, a short answer to each question reveals why standards-driven reform is necessary:

- *Where are we?* We are trapped in a time warp. Our schools were designed in the 19th century while we stand on the threshold of the 21st century.

- *Where do we want to be?* We want performance-driven schools to bring all Americans up to high standards.

- *How do we get there?* With painful self-examination and prodigies of hard work. Policies, practices and attitudes must undergo fundamental change.

Asking these questions again and again is essential, because their answers depend on context. And each step forward changes the context, just as external factors change it. The context of the 1990s and beyond — as far as we can see into the future — has three critically important dimensions.

- Education has never been more important, for citizenship, economic well-being, and personal growth and satisfaction. Without world-class schools, we are all in deep trouble. Until recently, there was a different education for each domain: citizenship, economic life and private life. No longer. Every child in America must be equipped with the knowledge and skills to understand our history, speak our language and prepare for an uncertain future. All Americans must have a common core of knowledge, and we cannot afford to leave anyone behind.

- Mastery, as evidenced by performance (outputs not inputs), will characterize the successful school of the future. From the earliest days of public education to the present, our schools have been "input-driven," described by what went into them, not what came out. No longer. Our best schools are already "output-driven," and the rest must become output-driven as well. Mastery is the metric of the future.

- Time has been the constant since the beginning of mass public education. Students got it within the time allowed or they didn't. No longer. In the school of the future, time will no longer be the fixed variable, and achievement will no longer be optional; time will be flexible, learning will be constant and all students will be held to high levels of achievement.

Ours is a society that thrives on change. We pay ceaseless lip service to it. But a hard truth remains. Most of us prefer "having changed" to "changing." And as John Murphy is fond of saying, when it comes to change, American schools have two speeds: slow and slower.

Do we offer these observations to frighten Sunday soldiers and would-be reformers? We do. Performance-driven school reform is not for the faint-hearted. Reform is hard work, and whoever embarks on the path does so at substantial risk. The road to performance-driven schools is fraught with peril; it is rocky and uneven. But there is a greater risk. Run no risk at all and you are assured of one thing: mediocrity.

Teachers are deeply skeptical about change. They've seen changes come and go — they've grown weary of the "reform of the month." Been there, done that. Indeed, like the survivor of trench warfare, the wise teacher has learned to keep his or her head down. Adding to the problem, change in school is typically imposed from on high. Only rarely are teachers partners in the change process; even less rarely are they permitted to initiate it. The beta sites chronicled in this book have broken this pattern. Each beta site in its own way is committed to democratic reform with a small "d"; it begins that way and it remains that way. Teachers and the community are not passive observers or advisors. They are participants. No longer objects of change, they are beneficiaries of change.

Places like **Charlotte-Mecklenburg, NC**; **Beaufort County, SC**; **Guilford, ME**; **Murfreesboro, TN**; and **Red Clay, DE**, are setting the pace. If they can do it …

# TAKE THE
# PLUNGE

## Building Public Demand For Standards and Reform

First things first. Before change comes ownership. The "build it and they will come" approach to school reform — where a few isolated individuals at the top institute change and convince others to support and institutionalize the improvements — doesn't work. That approach may create pockets of excellence, but they rarely transfer.

Enduring change and results require connecting a critical mass of education's stakeholders to a common vision from the start. Parents — and the broader community — make a huge difference in how much and how well children learn. Students come from and go home to adults. They grow up and spend time in neighborhoods. Both have more impact than educators sometimes like to admit. Estimates are that school takes up less than 10 percent of young-sters' lives. The rest of their time — a full 90 percent — is spent outside of school. Parents, churches, employers and other institutions are the custodians of that time. Their beliefs — the principles and values by which they live — set the tone for much of what goes on inside schools. The young watch their elders to gather clues about what's important, about how to live.

## TAKE THE PULSE OF YOUR COMMUNITY

Communities that hold scholastic achievement — and their school districts — in high regard encourage learners to excel amidst the many competing pressures, such as TV, clothes, cars, the cute kid across the hall. When communities don't value learning, children rarely do either. Unless a community unites to elevate the status of schooling, there is little chance for widespread improvement.

To successfully bring about change, the community must be convinced that change is both necessary and desirable. That means laying out the facts — all the facts, the good and not-so-good — which takes both wisdom and courage. Even if your school system by all indications is performing well in the aggre-gate, some students are not succeeding at high levels. They deserve attention. Moreover, check to see how your district is performing when measured against the world's best practices and best schools. That is your competition and your standard, not the neighboring district barely making it. In education, as in all areas of life, settle for things as they are and something will probably gain on you.

Building consensus, no matter the size of the community, takes time, goodwill and sound ideas. The process is as grueling as it is vital, but without it, change is slight and ownership nonexistent. While schools cannot do the job alone, they should make the first move, open the doors, throw up the shades and begin the dialogue. Parents and community members don't always understand they can get involved and have a say in the reform process.

David Mathews, former U.S. Secretary of Health, Education and Welfare and author of an important book, _Is There a Public for Public Schools?_, cautions school officials to be careful of the temptation to involve citizens simply as a means to ends that you already have in mind. The tendency in education — as in most public endeavors — is to provide people with ample opportunities to vent while the "professionals" take charge of developing the solutions. Sincere though the intent may be, this method is a public relations tactic, not a means of building genuine public support for schools. Being sold on what someone else has decided does not carry the same moral authority as owning the process.

Getting connected is key. Communities are collections of individuals who do not work as a community until they have a sense of their shared fate, overlapping goals and interdependence. As Mathews reminds us, people join in civic action when they understand how a problem affects what they care about, when they feel that solutions exist and when they feel others share their excitement about the possibilities.

## REFRAME THE ISSUES

School leaders: Get out from behind your desks and schedule a series of town meetings in quick succession to help set the stage and build excitement about the process of improving schools. Take time to reframe issues commonly referred to as "school problems" in terms of the larger context of community concerns. People don't normally link education and their community, yet public schools are the zone of intersection for every policy concern before the

_For more detailed discussion of standards, see Step 2._

_For more on community partnerships, see Step 7._

SPOTLIGHT

# DON'T ROUND UP THE USUAL SUSPECTS

How do you make sure that these community meetings have teeth? How do you get new blood into the process? Scour every sector of your community for people who are active and resourceful, for people who have a unique perspective and are interested in the welfare of the community, and for young people in particular.

Members of Beaufort 2000, the catalyst for change in **Beaufort County, SC**, did just that. Rather than rely on traditional mailing lists, filled with people who always serve on school system committees and attend board meetings, members took the initiative to knock on people's doors and solicit support. They watched the newspapers for "up and comers," activists and other talented people just moving into the community and for people who cared enough about the schools to make constructive comments in the "Letters to the Editor" column. Local business leaders and members of civic associations and professional organizations are good bets too, even though their focus may not seem to be on education. Such groups are brimming with talented, dedicated people eager to make a difference.

Make it clear that this is not one more informational meeting in which the revealed word is dispensed by all-knowing and all-seeing experts. The first step in a community dialogue that produces real results is action-oriented and genuine. Why? In part because the school community is charting *terra incognita;* accordingly, you really need each other. But real community dialogue is important in large part because you are embarked on a transformation that can only occur with broad participation and support. Your schools are going to change from institutions that are fixated on "inputs" to institutions that are determined to get "results" – real results using high, world-class, academic standards of performance. Such a change cannot be parachuted in from outside; it must grow organically in the community. "What your students know and can do" as a condition of graduation must, of necessity, reflect what the community believes.

voting public, from international competitiveness and readiness for work to teenage pregnancy and drug abuse prevention — not to mention high school football and school construction contracts.

If the issues remain narrowly focused on professional considerations, the broader community is uninterested and disengaged. For example, if you ask people what they think about the high school mathematics curriculum,

## SPOTLIGHT

# THE RIGHT QUESTIONS

Creating a "public" for education begins with identifying community problems, framing issues and creating a public space in which to talk. Pose these questions to members of your community, just as John Murphy did in his first weeks as **Charlotte-Mecklenburg, NC's** superintendent:

- What is valuable to your quality of life?

- What in your community is most valuable to you?

- Why is it so important?

- What do you want changed in this community?

- What do you want left alone?

- What moves will you support?

- What will you fight?

- What trade-offs are you willing (or unwilling) to make?

- Who do you get your information from? Do you have confidence in the source?

Ask the same questions about schools. The opportunity to talk plainly about the current condition of the community and the schools — and where both should be headed — gives everyone a personal stake in reforming the education system and provides the capacity for sustained improvement. The connections between the two become obvious to all who participate.

you're not likely to stir up much interest. But if you ask people if they know that the local economy is threatened by inadequate schools, you're more likely to capture their attention. In the same vein, questions about school discipline are related to larger questions about safety on the streets. Frame the issues that way. Make the connections between schools and the community; the links aren't always obvious to people. If you do so, sparking interest in what schools do won't be hard — provided the meetings are well publicized.

If someone is responsible for summarizing the opinions and issues, you can discern trends and determine what to do first. Responding immediately to concerns about safety and discipline, for instance, builds trust and respect. It convinces the public that the climb from input-driven to performance-driven schools is worthwhile.

One town meeting feeds the other. Dedicate a month to the effort. Hold town meetings at various dates, times and places to encourage wide participation. Listen to what's on the public's mind. The meeting is not a time for speeches, expert presentations or promotions of pet projects. School board members, the superintendent and key central office personnel should be on hand to hear what people have to say. Having the "top of the ticket" on hand signals to the community that these meetings are important.

## BUILD CAPACITY FOR SUSTAINED IMPROVEMENT

Change for the better is slow, just as is change for the worse. Traditional school planning tends to degenerate into a tug-of-war for authority, an "us-versus-them" mentality. Poor communication, mutual suspicion and unhealthy recriminations often define relationships: Parents blame the community for their children's problems, communities blame the school and the school frequently blames both. Everyone acts as if the task of improving the school belongs to somebody else. Before you know it, isolation sets in and the school is closed off from people who have a stake in and something valuable to offer to the learning enterprise.

## IN BEAUFORT

## BEAUFORT 2000 IS A CATALYST FOR CHANGE

Self-appointed and self-directed, Beaufort 2000 took to heart its self-imposed charge to become a force for change. The organization was made up equally of newcomers like Bonnie Smith from Michigan (now, three years later, a member of the school board); Norman Harberger, a human resources consultant with a penchant for statistics (formerly with a major chemical company and originally from Pennsylvania); and Bill Marsher, a third-generation native of Beaufort County (and a product of **Beaufort County, SC**, schools and the Massachusetts Institute of Technology). These community members looked closely at Beaufort's school system — and they did not like what they found.

They did find an abundance of goodwill, some excellent teachers and principals, and adequate buildings and grounds, but Beaufort's schools — like many around the nation — were not reaching world-class standards. They weren't even close. A 1952 Ford was a wonderful car in 1952; today it is an antique that won't go far or fast. The schools were as good as they had been — but that wasn't good enough to meet today's standards.

The members of Beaufort 2000 were not content to complain and present problems, however. To the contrary, they were convinced that solutions existed. They proposed one, brought to their attention by Alden Dunham, formerly education program officer for the New York–based Carnegie Foundation. After retiring to Hilton Head, Dunham discovered the standards work that **Charlotte-Mecklenburg, NC**, schools had completed. He secured written copies and substituted the name Beaufort for Charlotte-Mecklenburg. Simple, direct, economical. The process had one major drawback, however — it did not confer ownership, the key to standards. But if Charlotte could do it, so could Beaufort.

Schools cannot do the job alone. In the words of the late educator, Dr. Ernest Boyer, "We cannot have an island of excellence in a sea of indifference." If each of us acts as though the task belongs to somebody else, the transformation of the American school will remain out of reach. To put learning in America powerfully back on track, everyone has to work smarter, work harder and make sacrifices.

A 1993 report, *Divided Within, Besieged Without*, from **Public Agenda**, a New York–based nonprofit research organization that specializes in public attitudes about schools, provides a revealing look at the parochial turf fights that have derailed too many school improvement efforts around the country. "In all four communities [we studied], groups that should work together — groups that must work together if there is to be progress — seemed continually pulled apart by suspicion, prejudice, and fear of losing hard-won gains. In conversation after conversation, talk about long-term goals descended almost immediately into talk about local politics, local disputes, who did what to whom, and how to prevent it the next time around."

Powerful and enduring education change results from implementing new strategies and tactics on the one hand and building new, powerful decision-making structures on the other. Both the "what" and the "how" are crucial. Reform proposals, even ones that are superb, won't work if reformers are unable to master the process of change.

Town meetings are a first step and raise awareness. But deliberation — bringing people together over a sustained period of time, face-to-face, to examine a variety of perspectives and weigh the options — is key.

### Form a District Leadership Team

Larger districts should create a permanent leadership team with representation from all sectors to come together as equals to solve problems and champion the transformation process. The leadership team is not another layer of bureaucracy but an official body that can bring all the distinct voices of your community together in one room to develop a coherent vision to drive reform. (Small districts probably do not need to create a separate group.)

In addition to selected members of the school board and central administration, principals; teachers; parents; health and human service agencies;

## THE ISSUE OF SCALE

America's 15,025 school districts in 1993–94 range from the gigantic – such as New York City, with 1,005,521 students – to the tiny – such as Holt County District 231, NE, with two students. And no two districts are alike. But there are some general rules about organizing reform efforts in light of district size. The first rule is to involve as many citizens and educators as possible – easier to do in small districts. The second is to be realistic; if you can't get all your teachers in one room, think big. If you can get them all in one room, think small.

For example, when reform began in **Charlotte-Mecklenburg, NC**, which has 90,000 students in 118 schools, having a small, responsive and representative leadership team reporting to the superintendent

was clearly necessary. This also was true in Arizona and Pennsylvania, where state-wide efforts were undertaken. In smaller, more manageable communities like **Beaufort County, SC** (with nearly 15,000 students), and **Red Clay, DE** (with about 14,000 students), a district-wide leadership team would have been redundant. Existing district-wide connections completed the reform circle.

Much of the credit for the ground-breaking work in forming and sustaining district leadership teams belongs to a corps of Motorola executives led by Gail Digate. Over the past decade, they have perfected the leadership team process, working in conjunction with widely varying school district partners in the states of Illinois, Arizona and Massachusetts.

university, civic, religious and business leaders; and students should be asked to join the decision-making team. A leadership team should have at least 10 members and not more than about 20 to be manageable. Ask people to sign on for the long term to frame the questions, set the vision and direct the work processes of the school transformation effort.

As leadership team expert Gail Digate (former Motorola executive and current president of Leadership Learning Systems) instructs, provide your team with training on thinking strategically; building consensus; working as a team; solving problems; and using data, marketing and communications. Think about investing in an experienced facilitator to train your team to become self-directed. Key ingredients to team effectiveness are the existence of a well-defined mission, clear operating rules and agreement on decision-making procedures — all issues a trained facilitator can address.

It goes back to the wisdom outlined in the book, *Is There a Public for Public Schools?*: Teams whose members represent constituencies beyond traditional education boundaries yield better decisions. These teams level the playing field and encourage groups that are often at odds with one another to share ideas and assume personal responsibility for improvement. The deliberations that ensue allow people to drink in one another's experiences. The informality prompts a degree of candor. While participants may not change their own positions on an issue, their opinions of others' opinions often change — spawning new insights, new ways of seeing problems and new ways of acting together.

In **Murfreesboro, TN**, for example, a "Vision Committee" of about 20 people has been meeting for several months. The team's focus so far has been on issues of equity: Is the school district catering to four newer schools at the expense of older, inner-city schools? A tough question, but one that lays out the community's hot-button concerns and plays right into the future discussion of high standards for *all* students.

## Set Priorities

Although most of us are products of the education system, the business of schooling remains enigmatic. As many definitions exist as there are people, and none is very concrete. Energetic discussions about the definition of what your school system stands for and wants to produce serve to clarify and energize your reform effort. Giving members of the broader community authority to make changes heightens familiarity with and understanding of your system's problems and needs. Most important, it gives you a laboratory for innovation and invention. Any group tends to resist external demands; educators are no exception. But having teachers and administrators sit shoulder-to-shoulder with other citizens creates common ground. When all stakeholders take part in planning, selling the ideas to any group or groups is not necessary.

Finally, getting people talking helps to move the debate from things over which schools have little or no control to those over which they do. This process helps move past the self-defeating laundry list of "if only." *If only* we had more money, *if only* class sizes were smaller, *if only* students were better behaved and more motivated, *if only* drugs and violence didn't take such a toll, *if only* TV didn't have such a lock on students, *if only* parents were more involved in their child's education, we could make progress.

In districts or states that need leadership teams, the imperatives are straight-forward: Meet regularly and place children's needs first. Get to the heart of the issue — what quality of life do we want here and what role should schools play in making this happen? Worry more about what students require and less about what the system and the adults need. Worry more about what you want and less about what's wrong. Focus more on common-alties than differences. Emphasize the capacities in the schools and the community rather than the needs. If you label people or institutions only with the names of their deficiencies, you may miss what is most important: the opportunity to harness forgotten abilities, talents and resources. And be sure to encourage innovation and risk-taking. The adage, "If you always do what you always did, you will always get what you always got," should hang in the meeting room as a reminder.

Charting new directions is considered risky, yet sustained success is unreal-izable without change. Beyond that, prepare agendas and publish minutes of meetings. And supply your leadership team with quantitative and qualitative data, academic and otherwise, to guide its work. Information provides proper nutrition for a robust team. Without reliable data, no one can know whether schools are headed in the right direction, whether to adjust the course, and — vitally important — whether schools are succeeding.

Formation of a leadership team should come right on the heels of the town meetings, when momentum and interest are running high. If you are serious about doing business differently and engaging community partners, then do so immediately.

The leadership team's work should run to the heart of school operations. If you relegate it to the sidelines or portray it as a mere add-on or public relations scheme, the team loses its power, and the school district loses the benefit of its power.

## Develop a Mission Statement

Once the stakeholder group has gelled as a team, its first order of business is to focus the district on the "right stuff" — to straighten priorities and shift any preoccupation with buses, buildings and budgets to a preoccupation with academic standards and accountability. What are the objectives, pur-poses and directions of the system? What is our mission? What is our vision?

WORRY MORE ABOUT WHAT STUDENTS REQUIRE AND LESS ABOUT WHAT THE SYSTEM AND THE ADULTS NEED.

To direct the energies of your community, the vision should be grand and vivid enough to justify the struggle and specific enough to define the foundations and purposes of your new enterprise. It should capture the imagination of the publics of education and direct the energies of the organization. Tie it to high standards, high performance and the community's education goals (gleaned from the town meetings) and it's an easy sell to parents, business leaders and the broader community. Standards and accountability are "motherhood and apple pie" goals and hard to argue against. In keeping with the vision, the mission statement should rest on the belief that all youngsters have the natural ability to succeed at high levels and the responsibility of the schools is to find out how to nurture, develop and encourage each innate talent. No excuses allowed.

➤ **Sample mission statements**

## Develop Reform Principles

Beyond a mission statement, settle on principles to steer your course to its destination. No strategy, no style of operation should be allowed to stand unless faithful to the full set. Make the mission statements and organizing principles memorable. Get them down to a few pithy statements that everyone can understand. Once they are secured, the scope of team-driven decisions can run the gamut from standards to curriculum redesign, assessments, school organization, hiring and instructional delivery methods.

➤ **14 points of Charlotte-Mecklenburg's World Class Schools Panel**

## Organize Community Forums

Once your leadership team settles on a mission statement and vision, put both out for community review and comment. You want your central vision-building process to spark a whole series of intense discussions about renewal in the community to fuel the reform effort. The feedback you get from the forums will help sharpen your statement. Moreover, provided your mission and vision are on target, support will grow through the publication of your efforts. If experience is any guide, the ideas and opinions that surface will be remarkably consistent — but be open to differences in opinion.

Make sure the meetings include a broad range of people whose perspectives and experiences differ. Ask people from your community to gather as a focus group for a few sessions to sharpen the work of the leadership team.

Organize forums in any way that makes sense to your community. You may want to bring students together in one forum, teachers in another, parents in another and civic leaders in another to preserve the distinct voices of each. Or organize around natural geographic areas or school clusters in your community. Whatever the case, structure the forums to give people a real say-so. Like the town meetings, community forums are not a time for speeches or canned programs from the powers that be, while participants remain silent. Tailor the message to the needs, interests and perspectives of the forum members.

Set a time and location for the meetings that ensure a good turnout, such as early on weekday evenings at schools, libraries, town halls and recreation centers. (The site should have room to accommodate a large number of people as well as breakout rooms to handle small discussion groups.) Mix up the days and times to ensure a good turnout. Contact key community groups, such as your PTA and chamber of commerce, to solicit their ideas and to make sure your meetings do not conflict with other scheduled events. While you're at it, ask these and other key groups to send representatives and to get their members to attend the forums. Personal invitations and follow-up calls help boost attendance. When you can, make people personally responsible for bringing others to the forums.

Stay focused. After the introductions and a brief session to set the context for the meeting, get down to business. Divide people into small groups or teams of 10 to 12 members to encourage people to speak their minds, get creative and think big.

After a sufficient period for deliberation — a couple of hours at a minimum — ask each team to report to the larger group. Record the responses and develop a summary that reflects both the diversity and the areas of agreement.

Incorporate feedback. Use the summaries to guide your transformation efforts and adjust your vision accordingly. The leadership team is the perfect

**MAKE SURE THE MEETINGS INCLUDE A BROAD RANGE OF PEOPLE WHOSE PERSPECTIVES AND EXPERIENCES DIFFER.**

# STEP 1

COMMUNICATION
WITH THE
COMMUNITY
IS A TWO-WAY
STREET: IF
YOU ASK
QUESTIONS,
YOU MUST
LISTEN TO THE
ANSWERS AND
BE PREPARED
TO HONOR
SERIOUS
REQUESTS.

## TAKING DIFFERENT STEPS TO ROUSE THE COMMUNITY

Leadership teams and community-wide meetings are not the only ways to awaken complacent communities. Citizens in **Guilford, ME**, were roused by a bold move to change the *status quo*, which prompted people to sit up and take notice.

Norm Higgins, then high school principal and now superintendent, caused an uproar in 1988 when he required all students to take one semester of arts education in each of two fine arts disciplines, such as dance, drama, creative writing and visual arts. Band didn't count. "I was convinced arts education increased academic performance, created a different social mix in schools and added equity," he says. In blue-collar Guilford, parents balked. Guilford and the nation were still several years away from recognizing that creative thinking is critical in the workplace.

Higgins rejoiced: He had captured people's attention. In 1989, the Kennedy Center for the Performing Arts recognized the high school for its leadership in arts education. Today, arts education is part of Guilford's rigorous core curriculum.

vehicle to incorporate the feedback and report the results to the community via letters and the media. This process lets you breathe life into the new vision because it belongs to the entire community.

Communication with the community is a two-way street: If you ask questions, you must listen to the answers and be prepared to honor serious requests. In his first weeks as superintendent in **Charlotte-Mecklenburg, NC**, John Murphy discovered that the biggest community concerns were safety and busing. He could not in good faith ignore these issues, nor could he afford to do so politically. His reform agenda would have been fatally compromised. His magnet school program addressed both issues: choice for those who wanted it and alternative schools for students who couldn't function in regular schools.

# HOW GOOD IS GOOD ENOUGH?

## Organizing Around High Academic Standards

Imagine an America without standards — airline pilots who are long on enthusiasm but short on skills, self-declared brain surgeons high on self-esteem but low on technique, or unlicensed automobile drivers. It's a hair-raising vision, but exactly the situation we face in our nation's schools. What's missing are specific and measurable objectives for all students. High schools, for example, have a cornucopia of course offerings rather than a limited number of courses that must be mastered as a condition of graduation.

As a nation, we have avoided the basic decision about what students need to learn, and the results have not been good. Student promotions are based on attendance rather than mastery, and a host of reform efforts have done little to raise student achievement. Nothing is more dispiriting than a child who has completed 12 or 13 years of schooling and is unable to pass an Armed Forces qualifying exam, a letter carrier's exam or a Federal Express delivery driver's exam. No more frustrating experience confronts a dedicated teacher than witnessing social promotion. Unhappily, students can complete high school in the United States without being able to read, write and compute at useful levels.

## DEVELOP ACADEMIC CONTENT STANDARDS

### Keeping Your Eye on the Ball

High standards for graduation hold the promise to change all that. They help everyone keep their eye on the ball. First, standards specify what graduates are expected to know and be able to do as a condition of earning a diploma. Second, when satisfied, standards certify students' capacity just as standards of weights and measures provide accurate information about size.

Once communities agree about what students should learn, schools can dedicate their energies and resources to providing all students the opportunities to do the work: read and write better; perform well in mathematics, the

TO HAVE ANY
REAL EFFECT,
STANDARDS
MUST BE
INCORPORATED
INTO THE LIFE
OF THE
SCHOOL.

*Performance
standards and
assessments are
discussed further
in Step 5.*

sciences and the arts; speak other languages; and learn more about history, geography and civics. Once districts adopt and publicize standards, teachers, parents, taxpayers and children themselves will be clear about what students are expected to know and be able to do. All students, whether from wealthy or impoverished circumstances, with or without college aspirations, will be studying a challenging core curriculum. Teachers' roles will be strengthened because they will determine how best to meet the standards. Just as important, a written record of what's expected will exist against which to judge the progress of students and schools.

### Local Ownership Is Essential

Nationally, everyone is talking standards, but the debate remains largely unconnected to implementation. Reformers are ready to declare victory as soon as high and rigorous standards are adopted. The challenge for school districts is not simply to set standards but to *meet* standards. To have any real effect, standards must be incorporated into the life of the school. They must be embraced by the classroom teachers who must teach them, embraced by the students who must learn them, embraced by the parents who must support their children in learning them, and embraced by the business community and colleges that may or may not accept students as their next generation.

Setting rigorous standards in isolation will not work. The best product in the world — no matter how well conceived — is useless if it sits on a shelf unopened and unused. The bottom line is ownership. In real estate, it is location, location, location. In standards-based reform, it is ownership, ownership, ownership. Who sets the standards and how they are set are key — the process is as important as the product. A high-performance school cannot be imposed from the top down. It can't be parachuted in from Washington, DC, from a state or even from a central office. It must be homegrown to work; the community must take ownership if the reforms are to be more than cosmetic.

Nothing is more important to the life of the school; indeed, standards transform teaching from blue-collar work to professional work. They transform schools from *their* schools to *our* schools. Without ownership, teachers march to the beat of others' drums; they are not in control of their professional lives. When teachers and other stakeholders are deeply involved in the standards-setting process, they become both owners and professionals. What this means is that not every district will actually develop standards from scratch; to the contrary, only those on the leading edge will. **Charlotte-Mecklenburg, NC,** (not to mention the **New Standards**™ project) has done its work well. Its standards are there to see.

Early on in the standards-setting process, we need to be clear about a burning question: Why should an individual community set standards of excellence for its students when having national standards would be much more efficient?

Intellectually, the logic for one set of national standards is compelling. Ours is a continental democracy and common market, with a common language and common culture, characterized by extraordinarily high mobility rates. Although we differ from region to region, we are one people: *E pluribus unum.* Indeed, the modern public school that appeared in the mid-19th century was called the "common school." And in the 20th century, the average American moves once every five years, the highest mobility rate, by far, in the modern world.

All Americans have powerful reasons to refer to a common set of standards — not federal government standards, but national standards. No one has made a more compelling case for this than Diane Ravitch, a senior fellow at the Brookings Institution and former assistant secretary of education in the U.S. Department of Education. Why, then, do we propose building standards community by community, district by district, state by state?

The short answer is ownership. To be sure, education has a state, regional, national, even global dimension, but it is imparted locally. In an egalitarian democracy, with a long and jealously guarded tradition of local control, academic standards are not conferred by edict either from the state capitals or from Washington, DC. And even as standards should be national and international in scope, implementation has powerful local and regional dimensions.

Does this mean that there will be 50 sets of state standards or, worse, 15,025 sets, one for each district (plus another 25,000 sets for each of the nation's private schools)? Hardly. Convergence among the states and among school districts is natural and spontaneous. As standards work progresses, it will be clear that there is no Oregon mathematics and Florida mathematics, no Chicago chemistry and Nashville chemistry. Indeed, states such as California and private organizations such as the Thomas B. Fordham Foundation already are doing valuable work in comparing various sets of state standards — and making their assessments public. Every community can use these benchmark comparisons as a starting place. Each community's standards will be more alike than different. But that does not warrant imposing them on a community; to the contrary, the consensus among states and communities about what students should know and be able to do is all the more reason for standards to be accepted willingly at the local level.

The differences that will emerge, community by community, will be most apparent not in the standards but in curriculum and teaching units. These differences will be sensible and defensible. The standard that all students must be able "to read and comprehend a foreign dispatch in a major news magazine" can be satisfied by a dispatch from Kenya, China or Japan, and demonstration of mastery can be provided in a number of ways: a spontaneous oral presentation, an essay, a videotape and so on.

This is not, it must be stressed, an invitation to balkanization. Instead, it ensures ownership is where it belongs, at the local level, and actually increases

## IN BEAUFORT

# THE IMPORTANCE OF LEADERSHIP — FROM THE BOTTOM UP

Beaufort County, SC, had the ingredients — talent, energy and readiness to move — for a successful reform effort. However, it lacked a focal point. The district turned to national education reform leaders Lamar Alexander and David Kearns (both of whom had recently left the U.S. Department of Education as secretary and deputy secretary, respectively) and Charlotte-Mecklenburg, NC, Superintendent John Murphy. Inde-pendently, each of the three gave the same advice: Hire a consulting team to lead you through the wilderness. The school board and superintendent issued a Request for Proposals, received five bids and after interviewing two finalists, settled on Doyle Associates (DA). The team, headed by DA's principal, Denis Doyle, consisted of standards expert Susan Pimentel; Jeff Schiller and Dan Saltrick, then assis-tant superintendents for Charlotte-Mecklenburg; and Warren Simmons of the Philadelphia Education Fund.

Not surprisingly, DA's advice and the subsequent Beaufort experience are the basis for this book. The first order of business was to be dramatically democratic (with a small "d"). Diffuse leadership down. Turn to the community itself. This idea worked because the real

*continued on page 23*

the likelihood of securing real national standards. National standards will not be an elite enterprise, originating in Washington, DC; national standards will grow organically from local and state standards. The critical distinction is between the words "national" and "federal." To many people, they are synonymous. They are not. The genius of the framers of the U.S. Constitution was their commitment to the idea that government should be limited and as close to the people as possible. In no area of our communal life is this more important than in public education. To be sure, the federal government must support and defend constitutionally guaranteed civil rights in our schools, as well as elsewhere. But Uncle Sam does not have the intellectual, administrative or pedagogical capacity to make decisions about school operations.

## Defining Terms

If you're confused about the language of standards, you're not alone. On the next page is a sports analogy that is instructive for defining standards terms, a useful starting point for the work at hand.

*continued from page 22*

issue in school reform is ownership. The issues are only partly technical or professional; in large measure they are matters of vision and will. Standards committees, task forces, focus groups and public meetings were held with one purpose: to set world-class standards and hold the schools and the students to them. In the process, the community owned what it had created. Because the standards-setting process involved teachers and students as well as community leaders, the standards became theirs. Standards committees then took their work to the community as a whole — in community forums — and upon ratification, the standards went to the superintendent and school board, who also ratified them. The circle was complete.

Conventional school reform is parachuted in from the outside or imposed by a vigorous and visionary superintendent. Former Beaufort Superintendent Dick Flynn abandoned centralized reform and returned the process to the community.

This approach is effective because once the community is empowered to ask tough questions, an unswerving dedication to the reform process develops along with the conviction that the job can be done. In Beaufort, the most impatient and demanding citizens — whether on standards committees or the school board — won't rest until standards make their way into every classroom, changing, challenging and improving the education and life of every student in the Beaufort County public schools.

*1. Goal: Students are physically fit.*

A goal is the end result of a learning experience. A goal is often not measurable in an immediate sense. It reflects a state of being rather than a state of action. A goal reflects a purpose for instruction but does not designate the specific abilities that the learner will possess.

*2. Content (or exit) standard: 12-year-old students are able to run one mile. (A standard benchmarked to the President's Council on Physical Fitness.)*

A content standard supports the goal. It defines what students must know and be able to do — the knowledge and skills essential to meeting the goal.

A content standard, also known as an exit standard, is brief, crisp and to the point. It is written in jargon-free English so parents, teachers and children can understand it. The full set of content standards for a district should fit in a small loose-leaf binder, and a summary of them should pass the "refrigerator" test, as they do in **Beaufort County, SC**, and **Red Clay, DE**. (To pass the "refrigerator" test, the standards must fit on a chart that mom, dad or junior can post on the refrigerator); in Red Clay, each standard area (English, mathematics and so on) also passes the "bookmark" test. Boiled down, they fit on a bookmark!)

*3. Performance objectives: 12-year-old students understand the physiology of muscles, bones and the cardiovascular system; they are able to warm up and cool down safely; and they are able to pace themselves and breathe correctly while running.*

Performance objectives contain all the skills and knowledge a person needs to master the content standard. They detail the content standard. Educators may call performance objectives "further domain specification" or benchmarks as they describe the skills, habits and understandings that tests measure.

*4. Performance standards: 12-year-old boys are able to run one mile in 7 minutes, 11 seconds; 12-year-old girls, in 8 minutes, 23 seconds.*

Performance standards say how good is good enough to meet the content standard. They indicate how competent or adept a student demonstration must be to show attainment of the content standard. Without performance standards, a deliberate, unhurried stroll could constitute running a mile. Performance standards indicate the *quality of student performance* — is it acceptable, excellent or somewhere in between? Some districts also include the *nature of the evidence* (such as an essay, a mathematical proof, a scientific experiment or, in the case of physical fitness, running a mile) required to demonstrate that the content standard has been met.

Whether you look at passing scores for prospective doctors and lawyers on their respective boards or time trials for Olympic runners, achievement levels are set to motivate and measure performance. Olympic runners, for example, are not simply told they have to run fast to qualify for the 100-yard dash; they know exactly what times they need to beat. Performance standards define levels of performance, describing work at levels 1, 2, 3, 4 and 5; basic, proficient and advanced; or some other configuration.

### 5. Assessments or tests: 12-year-old students run one mile, demonstrating their ability to use proper form, and take a written test, demonstrating their understanding of the physiology of running.

Tests measure students' ability to meet the performance standard. Again, the performance standard specifies the student's degree of proficiency, defining what it means to run the mile in expert, advanced, competent or less-than-competent fashion.

### 6. Curriculum frameworks: These set out units on physiology, questions and topics to cover; suggested reading material; and training sessions needed to help 12-year-olds run one mile.

Curriculum frameworks are best characterized as descriptions of what should take place in the classroom; they flesh out in greater detail the topics, themes, units and questions contained within the standards. They are guides for teachers that address instructional techniques, recommended activities and modes of presentation. They describe how and in which grades and in what courses the essentials detailed in the content standards are to be taught. They name the textbooks, materials, activities and equipment that can best help students achieve the standards.

Unlike standards, curricula can vary — from state to state, city to city, even school to school — provided they focus on delivering the "big" ideas and concepts that a set of standards requires students to understand and apply. The animals, plants and ecologies students study in Miami may differ from those studied in Phoenix or New York, but the scientific concepts — natural selection and diversity, photosynthesis, energy movement and change in living organisms — are the same.

**BECAUSE TEACHERS ARE THE ONES WHO DELIVER THE STANDARDS, THEY SHOULD HAVE THE LOUDEST VOICE.**

## Form Standards-Setting Teams

**Select a cross-section of participants.** To develop a set of content standards, we recommend you bring, at a minimum, six kinds of people together: seasoned teachers who know firsthand the daily work of teaching; university scholars who are well versed in the content area and familiar with international demands; business and community leaders who know the skills needed in the marketplace; and parents and students who have a keen personal stake in what is taught. To have enough of a cross section, we recommend that each standards-setting team have 19 members and a teacher majority.

Because teachers are the ones who deliver the standards, they should have the loudest voice. Involving teachers deeply is symbolically and literally important. In **Beaufort County, SC**, and **Red Clay, DE**, each standards committee — English, science, mathematics, foreign language and history — was made up of 19 members: 10 teachers (three elementary, three middle and four high school), two parents; two content scholars; two business leaders; one school administrator; and two students. Teachers need to be freed up from some of their regular duties to take on this extra work. Be sensitive that many prefer to meet in the late afternoon rather than miss prime teaching time during the morning.

Team members need to come together as equal partners right from the start. The varied perspectives promise a richer product. Students really give the process starch. Without fail, they and their business counterparts are the toughest and most demanding committee members, challenging teams to break free from the *status quo* and to set standards that require all students to stretch.

**Cast a wide net.** Member selection can be varied. Although handpicking some members ensures the right mix of expertise and perspective, we suggest opening the process to add new voices and to avoid charges of elitism or committee "stacking." Get a true cross section of ages, genders, geographic areas and races and include the movers and shakers in each community — especially respected scholars and master teachers at the elementary, secondary and post-secondary levels.

**Set up a separate design team for each content area.** This makes the work more manageable and allows more people to take part than asking a single group to define the standards across the board. Organizing teams by content areas also is better than organizing around interdisciplinary learning goals (such as developing purposeful thinkers, effective communicators, self-directed learners, responsible citizens and creative problem-solvers). Some districts prefer interdisciplinary teams because real-world problems don't come in tidy bundles of mathematics, science or history. Our experience, however, is that when districts abandon the disciplines, standards suffer. They become vague, loosely constructed statements that lack depth and integrity.

**Look for the best in the world.** The design teams' first charge is to identify world-class standards — not minimal competencies — and to tailor them for their students. Content standards should set out what is most worth knowing and being able to do in the best traditions of a strong liberal arts education. Standards should establish what children should know, not how they are taught or measured. That said, standards need to reflect sensible criteria for usefulness, intelligibility, rigor and measurability. They need to focus on academics, contain the right mix of skills and content and represent a reasonable pattern of cumulative learning that is manageable given the constraints of time. In addition, standards should not inflame anyone's sensibilities.

Design teams can lean heavily on the expectations of several national (not federal) reform efforts and those within the **International Baccalaureate** and **Advanced Placement** programs — top American standards. Team members should feel free to pore through national, state and district standards, mixing and matching and strengthening them to more accurately reflect local expectations. National standards exist in the arts, civics, economics, English, foreign languages, geography, health, history, mathematics, physical education, science and social studies. Some are good, some are not so good. To quote Alex Haley, "Find the good and praise it." We add, "Discard the rest." Many of the national documents are voluminous; you'll need to practice courageous deletion.

> **Resource list for content standards**

> **Full text of standards from Beaufort County, SC; Colorado; Delaware; and Virginia**

One caution: Setting standards is stressful business. It signals big change and creates anxiety in people who have to meet tougher standards. Because

**BENCHMARKING THE DRAFT STANDARDS TO WORLD-CLASS LEVELS AND REVIEWING THEM FOR RELEVANCY, INTELLIGIBILITY AND MEASUR-ABILITY IS CRITICAL.**

"dumbing down" existing standards can be tempting, the ironclad rule is that new standards must have, at a minimum, the depth and rigor of the existing standards used as resources. Again, benchmarking the draft standards to world-class levels and reviewing them for relevancy, intelligibility and measurability is critical.

Review foreign documents. Finding out what the competition is doing is good practice. The most successful businesses dedicate whole divisions to tearing apart the most successful products on the market to gather clues on what makes them work. The intention isn't necessarily to reproduce every feature but to determine how to get their products to measure up. As the **American Federation of Teachers** (AFT) states in *World-Class Standards: How to Get There From Here*:

> If we don't [look at internationally competitive standards], there is a danger that those of us who have been involved so long in the struggle to raise student achievement will become prisoners of the *status quo*, unable to imagine youngsters achieving at higher levels than we are accustomed to. In this sense, our own experience can be limiting. The current emphasis on world-class standards is designed to free us from these limitations and biases, and encourage us to learn from the experiences of other countries. By looking at what students in other nations are capable of accomplishing, we may aim higher when judging the potential of our own youngsters.

Curriculum frameworks, syllabi, exams, textbooks and examples of student work reveal with precision and clarity what students in other countries are expected to learn. With these materials in hand, teachers and other stakeholders can see the expectations for themselves, and they can begin to ask and answer their own questions. The AFT recently released a report containing translated exams from France, Germany and Scotland. Another report compares the science exams taken by college-bound students in France, Germany, Japan and England. (The Mathematical Association of America and the National Endowment for the Humanities also have made useful translations of foreign curricula and exams.)

➤ **Resource list of foreign curricula and exams**

**Make sure the key issues are on the table.** When design teams first meet, expect heated debate and dialogue. Expect such questions as, "How can we set high standards when our students can't learn what we're teaching them now? You mean *all* students will be held to these standards, from the gifted and talented to those with special needs? All students are going to take algebra, geometry and some calculus? Sounds great, but who's going to give us the resources to make the changes? Who will train the teachers? Who will give teachers time to train and plan? Will someone be creating new assessments because the current ones won't be able to measure mastery of this level and complexity of material? Can you assure me that if I teach to the standards, my students will do well on the state assessments? How are you going to hold high school students to these high standards when most don't have an adequate foundation?"

Representation from the central office is key here. That way people can ask their questions and get straight answers. So be prepared.

Standards setters are reassured, and the conversations really take off if you address just how teachers will be trained; the role parents, business and higher education will play in maintaining high standards; the interventions and supports that will help students reach the standards; and the connections between the curricula and the exams.

Welcome the questions and the debate. Giving people the opportunity to say their piece allows them to vent their frustrations, grapple with the issues that matter most, broaden their thinking and coalesce as a team. Unless you confront the confusion and the anger in a meaningful way, you cannot release the seeds of creativity. Through deliberation and dialogue, team members will begin to understand that their charge is not to figure out why standards can't be achieved or, for that matter, how to achieve the standards. Design teams have but a single charge: to lay before the students, parents, teachers and the broader community a common core of learning that all students in a modern democracy have the right to confront. Period.

**Immerse teams in the process.** By rolling up their sleeves, wrangling over what setting standards means and phrasing standards (some groups debate a single sentence for an hour or more), teams form an unmistakable *esprit de corps*. Team members own the standards and champion their implementation

START WITH
THE BASICS:
READING,
WRITING,
SPEAKING AND
LISTENING, AND
MATHEMATICS.

in schools. Make no mistake, process is as important as the final product. When teachers and others get the idea that central administration is genuinely committed to the effort, excitement builds around the possibilities. Teachers recognize the promise: Standards provide them with an unprecedented opportunity to practice their craft, strut their stuff and divulge their expertise.

**Have expert facilitators on hand.** People who have been through the standards-setting process once or twice can help each design team with its work. One highly effective method is to name co-chairs of standards-setting teams, including at least one teacher from the school system. In a session or two, have the experts "train" the co-chairs on how to lead the standards-setting process — both in what makes a good standard and in effective facilitation strategies. People known and respected in the school community have instant credibility. The hurdle of an outside expert's "proving himself or herself" to a group is avoided. The experts then can serve as troubleshooters and aides to group leaders.

**Take time for critical review.** Give feedback to design teams as they move through the process. Having an independent set of eyes review their work helps make the standards rigorous, measurable and intelligible. National standards experts, content scholars, assessment experts or some combination of the three are perfect candidates to review the standards as they progress. The teams need to set a protocol for reviewing the content standards to ensure consistency in the reviews.

**Decide which content areas to cover.** Some districts limit themselves to mathematics, language arts, the natural sciences, history and geography. Others also set standards for foreign language, the arts, economics, health and physical fitness, workplace and computer skills, community service, and character education.

Most communities aren't sure where to begin. We recommend that you start with the basics: reading, writing, speaking and listening, and mathematics. Add other subjects as you progress and gain confidence. Some districts want to roll with everything at once, but logistical considerations may convince you to do your work in phases. **Beaufort County, SC**, staggered start dates: Three sets of standards committees began every month for three months in fall 1994; they reported results in a marathon session of meetings in one week in spring 1995.

Again, districts need not start from scratch. **Charlotte-Mecklenburg, NC,** used the **International Baccalaureate** exit standards and some national standards as starting points. **Beaufort County, SC,** used Charlotte-Mecklenburg's standards as a starting point, adjusting them as they deemed necessary. **Guilford, ME,** organized around Maine's Common Core of Knowledge, laying out the knowledge, skills and attitudes expected in four "new" content areas: the human record, communications, personal and global stewardship, and reasoning and problem-solving. Guilford wanted to signal a change to a new world order, but the familiar academic content areas are, of course, embedded in its standards. **Red Clay, DE,** used Delaware's academic standards as a benchmark.

**Backward mapping.** One secret of success in setting standards is "backward mapping." Once the standards committees decide what high school graduates should know and be able to do, they work backward to lower grades to map out a logical sequence of benchmarks. If all graduates should master algebra and geometry, speak a foreign language, write a persuasive exit essay or make a compelling verbal presentation, teams need to figure out what is appropriate in kindergarten, and in subsequent grades, to achieve these objectives.

**Settle on a single format.** Unless you use a common format, the end product is likely to be confusing and difficult to use. The national models — which together total more than 2,000 pages and weigh about 14 pounds and have their own formats and sets of definitions — discourage parents and students, not to mention teachers, from using the standards. You can offer a particular format or give standards writers a choice and then spend some time gaining consensus from the design teams. If you have the time, give teams a say over format. It's a good way for teams to get comfortable with the task and with each other.

For consistency's sake, though, write the standards in the same verb tense and reach agreement on paragraph form, bullet form, overarching standard statements, sample work and glossary. Setting a guideline on the number of pages sounds arbitrary, but it gives standards writers a sense of how detailed to get. That, in turn, helps to ensure some consistency across disciplines and protects against voluminous documents.

**Determine benchmark levels.** We favor organizing standards by developmental stages (or grade clusters) rather than by each grade level because it's a first step to breaking the arbitrary age–grade link that defeats so many students today. Build a system that can flex: Students can advance quickly through some subjects and slowly through others. Under such a system, the time required for a particular subject will differ by child, by interest and by skill, but whoever the child, the core learning expectations must stay the same.

In place of grade levels, districts such as **Charlotte-Mecklenburg, NC**, and **Beaufort County, SC**, and the state of Arizona have arranged skills and knowledge into five developmental levels:

- readiness, for preschool work

- foundations, for work through grades three or four

- essentials, for work through grade eight

- proficient, to graduate from high school

- distinction, for honors work

> **Beaufort's developmental-level definitions**

These benchmark levels provide flexibility while maintaining accountability. Many of the national models set standards for grades four, eight and 12; some states have added a readiness level and an advanced level. What's important is that all the teams in a district agree on the benchmark levels.

**Vary the presentation for each audience.** Computers make it easy to present the standards in several different ways. Parents may prefer to see the content standards organized by developmental or grade levels. That means seeing at a glance what it means to master mathematics (number sense and measurement, algebra, plane and solid geometry, probability and statistics, calculus) at the fourth-grade level as distinct from the eighth- and 12th-grade levels.

Teachers often prefer to see the information presented across the grades. A matrix that displays the developmental or grade levels down a vertical axis and the discrete areas (geometry, algebra, probability and statistics, number sense, and measurement) along the horizontal axis allows you to incorporate both views at a glance.

> **Examples of how standards can be presented to different audiences**

## USE THE RIGHT CRITERIA FOR A GOOD STANDARD

Not all standards are created equal. Vague, mushy standards that do not challenge students are worse than no standards at all. The good news — and bad news — is that targets set are likely to be met. American education made a major blunder in earlier decades by organizing thresholds around the lowest common denominator — usually defined as what every sixth grader should know. Minimum requirements fast turned into maximum goals. In the words of a **Charlotte-Mecklenburg, NC**, teacher, "No one rises to low expectations. Aim low, achieve a little. Aim high, achieve a lot."

What follows are some guideposts to set your review protocols. They have evolved from the early work of standards "greats" Paul Gagnon, a noted authority, Matt Gandal of the **American Federation of Teachers** (AFT), and Chester E. Finn, Jr., former assistant secretary of education, the John M. Olin Fellow at Hudson Institute and president of the Thomas B. Fordham Foundation.

**Rigorous.** Are standards sufficiently rigorous to be labeled "world-class"? Do they reflect internationally benchmarked standards, such as those on which **Advanced Placement** and **International Baccalaureate** programs of study are based? Do they reflect levels of knowledge and skills comparable to what students in high-achieving countries are expected to master? Do they reflect what the "best" students in the "best" American schools are studying? Do they set levels of desired performance as targets? Higher aspirations for everyone?

Answering these questions with certainty takes time. As a nation, we need to measure how our students fare on international comparisons over time and be prepared to update standards regularly. The bottom line, however, is that "world-class" means setting high expectations for all students that equal those of the best schools in other modern countries and the best schools at home. That means teaching *all* students what the "smart" kids in our best schools are learning today — a taller order than one might think. Only an estimated 20 percent of the nation's students take higher-level mathematics and science courses such as algebra, geometry and physics; only 30 percent master rigorous reading and writing courses; and about the same low percentage take any foreign language at all.

IF THE
KNOWLEDGE
AND SKILLS
CONTAINED
WITHIN
STANDARDS
CAN'T BE
ASSESSED,
THEY LOSE
THEIR
AUTHORITY.

Team members must be warned against falling into the trap of writing standards that reflect what is presently being taught. If standards are low, nothing will change, and student achievement will remain flat. For many teams, what helps is thinking about what a new group of students just entering school should know and be able to do by the time they graduate. It tends to free teams from getting locked in the box of what "is." Aligning standards to the admissions standards at four-year universities is another good strategy. Rigor means teaching demanding courses early.

**Valuable.** Do the standards address knowledge and skills that will be valuable over a student's lifetime?

If team members can't explain a standard to students or adults, revamp it or drop it. Including students on design teams will help to ensure relevance. Expect them to demand good reasons for a standard.

**Intelligible.** Are standards clear enough for teachers to understand what is required of them? Are standards written in jargon or are they clear enough for parents to keep an eye on their children's progress?

If a standard leaves people scratching their heads, rewrite it. Here are some examples of what to avoid:

- Students understand human development theories across the life span and value individual uniqueness in the context of family life.

- Students demonstrate knowledge and understanding of the variables influencing the effectiveness of the components of the communication process.

The task is not easy. Mathematics, for example, poses a particular challenge. If the language of mathematics is not included, rigor may be sacrificed. Writing mathematics standards in definite terms — even if they are not fully understood — will go a long way toward making the standards understandable to parents, students and the community. They may not know what it means, for instance, to "analyze Euclidean transformations, use simulations to estimate probabilities or analyze the parameter changes on functions," but parents armed with a copy of the standards can ask the teacher whether their children have mastered transformations, probabilities and functions. They can go further and ask the teacher to show them samples of student work. For their part, students will know whether or not they are learning what the standards say they are supposed to be learning. If students don't understand something in a standard at their developmental level, that's a good sign it hasn't been taught or hasn't been taught properly. In any case, define your terms. Add a glossary if you must. If necessary, less-technical versions of the standards can be written. You want the standards to be within reach of students, parents and community members.

**Measurable.** Are standards demonstrable and subject to assessment? Do they use verbs such as "demonstrate," "analyze," "explain," "compare," "identify," "describe," "compose" and "apply" that indicate an assessable action?

Many vital skills can't be captured in a pen-and-paper test — some are even difficult to measure with essays or other demonstrations — just as some skills that are easily measured aren't worth learning. But if the knowledge and skills contained within standards can't be assessed, they lose their authority in short order. Examples of standards that aren't measurable include:

- Students exhibit curiosity and the habit of lifelong learning.

- Students find satisfaction in reading and writing and make those activities part of their everyday lives.

- Students appreciate reading books representing different cultures and historical eras.

- Students respect past and present contributions of various language dialects to standard English.

It's not that teachers shouldn't try to pass on the joy of reading — the point is to measure proficiency in reading, not joy. Even if you could measure such concepts, would you even want to? To measure the first example — lifelong learning — one would have to delay measurement until a student was 80 years old. For the second and third, one would have to invent a joy meter of some sort, measuring smiles, giggles and appreciation. Standards such as these are more reminders to teachers about how they should teach rather than standards about what students should know and be able to do.

**Specific.** Are standards overly prescriptive? Overly general? Are the standards specific enough to guide teachers, curriculum and assessment developers, and others in their work?

# STEP 2

VAGUE, MUSHY
STANDARDS
THAT DO NOT
CHALLENGE
STUDENTS ARE
WORSE THAN
NO STANDARDS
AT ALL.

No one formula exists. But to determine if you are on the right track, team members can ask these questions: Are expectations for students at different developmental levels clearly stated? Are the standards clear and specific enough to guide the development of curriculum frameworks so that students can move with ease from district to district or school to school without having to play catch-up? Can textbook publishers and assessment developers use the standards for their work? Would the test and the standards be well aligned? Do the standards tell potential employers and colleges precisely what students will know and be able to do as they take them on as workers and students? Take these examples and compare:

**Weak, general standard**

- Students understand economic principles and are able to make economic decisions that have consequences in daily living.

**Strong, specific standard**

- Students assess the likely causes of the Depression and analyze its effects on ordinary people in different parts of the nation.

Note how the first example leaves the reader asking, "What economic principles? What economic decisions?"

**Weak, general standard**

- Students formulate and solve problems [What kind? Addition, division, algebra, calculus?] and communicate [How?] the mathematical processes [What processes? Theorems? Equations? Calculators?] and the reasons for using them.

**Strong, specific standard**

- Students understand and apply the basic geometric concepts of undefined terms, angle relations, perpendicularity, parallelism and inequalities.

**Weak, general standard**

- Students understand, analyze and interpret historical events [Which events?], conditions [What conditions?] and trends [What trends?].

**Strong, specific standard**

- Students explain the causes and effects of World War II, in terms of territorial aggression; rise of totalitarianism; the Holocaust and its impact; major battles, military turning points and key strategic decisions; and changes in the political map of Europe.

**Weak, general standard**

- Students read high school-level texts [What texts? For what purpose?] written by different authors [What authors?].

**Strong, specific standard**

- Students compare historically or culturally significant works of literature that express a universal theme and draw conclusions about the ways in which the content (i.e., key themes, patterns, ideas, perspectives) reflects the perspective of the author and the era during which he or she lived.

- Students evaluate public documents for the power and logic of the arguments advanced, the author's insight and foundations of support, the use of persuasive techniques, and the appeal to audiences both friendly and hostile to the position presented.

**Weak, general standard**

- Students use the correct forms of personal and public writing [What forms? To what level?] for a variety of purposes and audiences [What purposes? What audiences?].

**Strong, specific standard**

- Students write a persuasive essay that engages the reader; presents a definite point of view; and fully develops the view with powerful and pertinent facts, evidence, illustrations, arguments and descriptions.

On the other hand, standards can be overly prescriptive and speak to how standards are to be taught or students are to learn. Watch for teaching tools, exercises and activities. Here are some examples:

- Students listen to fiction and nonfiction texts read aloud.

- Students participate in formal/informal book talks.

- Students make up stories that go with number sentences.

- Students gather and analyze data from the neighborhood and compare the data with published statistics for the city, state or nation.

- Students create a mathematical real-life situation using functions and predict how it is affected by changes in information.

- Students analyze selected newspapers and magazines for accuracy and clarity of graphical presentations of data.

**Comprehensive.** Are the standards complete? Do they cover the subject in adequate breadth and depth? Do standards contain the major concepts of a field, the essential ideas that students must master if they are to have a grasp of the field?

Watch for obvious holes. For example, mathematics standards that don't cover algebra and geometry; English standards that don't adequately cover literature, grammar and how to write in different genres; or geography standards that don't cover how physical processes shape the Earth's systems and the physical and human characteristics of places.

**Academic.** Do standards focus primarily on academics — reading, writing, mathematics, science, history, geography, literature, and the arts — or do they focus overwhelmingly on social and behavioral issues?

For example, these standards do not focus on academics:

- Students understand their worth as individuals, exhibit self-esteem and work cooperatively with their peers.

- Students demonstrate the ability to accept responsibility for personal decisions and actions.

- Students demonstrate self-confidence and a willingness to risk mistakes in order to learn.

- Students have skills that enhance their personal well-being.

- Students demonstrate caregiving skills.

Such statements make people uncomfortable and can quickly derail any effort to set standards. Parents often feel that these invade their province. Moreover, proponents of these statements need to think carefully about the implications of including these as part of their standards document. Do you really want to fail someone who demonstrates poor self-confidence or low self-esteem? Leaving such statements out of your standards doesn't mean that schools don't have a role to play in helping students develop sound traits and strong characters. In fact, these statements often are included to remind teachers of their importance. They are in fact a natural by-product of a rigorous curriculum. As students learn about the conflicts and struggles for freedom, the heroes and villains, the debates and deliberations that have stirred mankind through the centuries and as students weigh the great controversies and compromises of history, they can't help but have their moral compasses tuned. So too, the act of interpreting literary texts enables students to participate in other lives, in worlds beyond their own, and to glimpse human motives and reflect on who they are in mind and will and spirit. Consider the content areas of science and foreign language and it becomes clear that each discipline offers its own brand of wisdom.

**Balanced.** Do standards cover both skills and knowledge? Do they speak of skills in the abstract or are they tied to important content?

Watch out for standards that speak exclusively of skills with no content knowledge in sight. For example, these standards are based on skills, not content:

- Students demonstrate the ability to think critically, creatively and reflectively in making decisions and solving problems.

- Students use imagination freely and effectively using a variety of complex reasoning processes including comparing, classifying, analyzing, problem-solving, investigating and abstracting.

Knowledge is dynamic, even transient, but how does one think critically, creatively and reflectively without thinking about something concrete? How is it possible to decide, analyze, investigate, compare or classify without content? Skills can't be taught in the abstract. Neither can they be assessed. Knowledge is the scaffolding upon which critical thinking is built.

**Manageable.** Are the standards manageable given the constraints of time, or do they contain ridiculously long sets of objectives that would leave teachers rushing lickety-split through material without proper emphasis or focus?

Standards shouldn't try to cover everything. Aim for no more than about 80 percent of the academic curriculum. Any more and you preclude individual schools and teachers from imprinting the standards with a personal touch. Americans spend about half as much time on academics as their counterparts overseas, so we have a way to go before we hit that wall. Nevertheless, there undoubtedly will be competing demands for time both within and among disciplines, so select information scrupulously. If a set of standards includes teaching activities and other "how-to's," they should be for illustrative purposes only.

**KNOWLEDGE IS THE SCAFFOLDING UPON WHICH CRITICAL THINKING IS BUILT.**

Later, through curriculum frameworks, teachers can make the most of opportunities for student work to do double and even triple duty, by forging stronger connections among subject areas through the way students are taught. For example, students could be asked to write a historical investigation research paper to satisfy both writing and history standards.

**Cumulative.** Are standards developmentally sound? Do they include a natural progression of learning? Is a proper foundation set at earlier levels to prepare students for more rigorous study at later levels? Is learning level to level well differentiated? Watch for repetitions of knowledge and skills at all benchmark levels. Saying students "know more" or are performing at higher levels is not useful. Nor is it useful to say students read at developmentally appropriate levels. Write standards so that the concepts mastered in previous levels form a base for students' comprehensive knowledge. That way, the information at one level need not be repeated at each succeeding level. Articulating subject matter from preschool through high school and beyond will do much to end the plague of repetitions, saving time and sparing students the boredom that often ensues from having to learn the same things again and again.

One caution: Sometimes when educators charge that the standards are "developmentally inappropriate," it may be code for, "The standards are too rigorous."

## BUILD COMMUNITY CONSENSUS

Once the teams are satisfied that the standards are high and real, take them to a community meeting and present them to citizens for their comment and input. Three levels of review are necessary:

**School and staff.** Teachers and principals throughout the district should be given time to review and comment. Groups of elementary, middle and high school teachers should review all the standards across the disciplines to ensure what's being asked of students is of consistent rigor and complexity and that proper foundations of knowledge are laid before moving on.

**Stakeholders.** Local employers should review the standards to make sure they include the work skills and knowledge they believe are essential. College deans and admissions officers should review the high school exit standards against their admission standards. Scholarly organizations at the local level as well as teacher associations should be invited to review the standards.

**Community.** Don't underestimate the wisdom of community members. Set a deadline and invite comments in writing. Hold community forums. Whether the forums are conducted in small or large groups, design team members should be on hand to explain the standards. The only rule for reviewers is the same as for design team members: They can suggest changes to make the standards *more* rigorous, but not less. Design teams can then reconvene to review the comments and make needed changes.

## Territorialism and Standards

Gaining ownership can be as messy as it is important. Many animals are highly territorial. People are no different; they have the same drive to "mark" their territory with complaint and criticism. Steel yourself. Do not get defensive. Take the criticism on the chin, stay calm and get beyond the outrage. Beneath the torrent of complaints often lie legitimate concerns or suggestions about how to improve the standards. If you can, view the negativity as a positive sign: You have succeeded in engaging your public. Work with them and the critics become your staunchest supporters. Arriving at usable descriptions of the knowledge and skills you want students to learn and forming a consensus around them take time. Get set for a number of rounds of revision and refinement — and a lot of hard work.

Once ownership roots, change is immediate. Schools can begin to organize around the standards. (Without widespread acceptance, the standards will be dead on arrival.) Depending on how often team members can meet and how much time team members can spare, districts can create their product in as little as six months. But setting a year's timetable to work out all the kinks and gain firm consensus from your community is probably prudent.

Over time, teachers recognize themselves, their goals and their daily endeavors in the document; they also are inspired, motivated and provoked to reevaluate some of what they do in class. Because disciplines continue to evolve and grow, standards that are developed must remain provisional enough to leave room for future developments in their respective fields. Without such revisions, standards soon will become artifacts of the age rather than enduring guideposts for

**GET SET FOR A NUMBER OF ROUNDS OF REVISION AND REFINEMENT — AND A LOT OF HARD WORK.**

**PERFORMANCE
OBJECTIVES
BRIDGE THE
GAP BETWEEN
DISTRICT EXIT
STANDARDS
AND THE DAILY
WORK OF
CLASSROOM
TEACHING.**

improving instruction. A final standards document in loose-leaf binders with margins for comments reminds people that the standards belong to the entire school community and require constant attention and comment.

## OVERHAUL THE CURRICULUM

### Develop Performance Objectives

Content standards set out what is most worth knowing and being able to do. They are meant to be scrupulously brief. Performance objectives — the next step — are meant to be longer and more detailed. They are the content standard in greater detail. Performance objectives bridge the gap between district exit standards and the daily work of classroom teaching. (The need for performance objectives depends on the specificity of your standards. If you set standards grade by grade with necessary detail, skip this step and move on to setting performance standards and assessments.)

Writing performance objectives needs to follow directly on the heels of standards-setting. Without clearly defined specifications, teachers and students remain distracted by courses and activities spilling out in all directions, in no discernible order of importance. Without definition, relevant, valid assessments remain out of reach.

When performance objectives are set, they should leave wide-open spaces for teachers to fill in with lessons of their choice. They should be specific enough to allow teachers to improvise and general enough not to get in the way of good teaching. Classroom teachers, who know their students best, need to decide which material to handle quickly and which material to handle in depth. They should decide on the topic sequence to lay out over the year and what books and materials will be most helpful to their students. Teachers know best what, if any, information to add to the list and what teaching methods to apply. Performance objectives provide a road map for teachers to follow. The objectives should:

- describe the *results* of learning rather than teaching strategies or learning activities;

- include performances that are relevant indicators for the capability to be learned; and

- include indicators of all critical aspects of the knowledge or skill to be learned.

## AN EXAMPLE OF PERFORMANCE OBJECTIVES

If a middle-school standard reads, "Students use correct punctuation, capitalization, grammar and usage, along with varied sentence structure and paragraph organization," the performance objectives might include: Students ...

- use colons to separate hours and minutes, to introduce a list and in business letters; semicolons between two clauses of a compound sentence not joined by a conjunction; and quotation marks around exact words of a speaker and names of poems, songs, short stories, etc.;

- capitalize sentence beginnings, titles, abbreviations, proper nouns, geographical names, holidays, historical periods, special events, magazines, newspapers, names of organizations and the first word in quotations;

- use correct verb tense including present perfect, past perfect and future perfect tenses; subject–verb agreement with compound subjects; and pronoun–antecedent agreement;

- use compound, complex and compound–complex sentences and effective coordination and subordination of ideas to express complete thoughts; and

- reinforce coherence within and across paragraphs by using parallel structures to highlight and reinforce main ideas.

**Ask teachers to take charge of this effort.** Teachers are best equipped to begin translating exit content standards into detailed performance objectives. To preserve continuity, ask teachers from the original standards-writing teams to take charge of the effort. At the same time, to increase ownership, it makes sense to add dozens of teachers to the performance objective-writing teams, representing every school in the district. Enlist others to review their work and still others to correlate the performance objectives to state-mandated tests. When the performance objectives go out under the names of dozens of teachers, they hold sway with the rest of their colleagues. Such a document is infinitely more credible than one written by the central office staff and dropped into schools.

Teams need to decide whether to build an entirely new set of performance objectives or adapt existing curricular documents. The answer may differ by content area. In some cases, the answer may be a little of both. Curricula used in the **International Baccalaureate** and **Advanced Placement** programs and other higher-level science, mathematics and literature courses can be adapted easily for all students — provided those programs of study correlate with the exit standards. To ensure all students have the proper foundation, teachers can backward map from these high-level performance criteria to include what students need to learn at the earliest grades forward.

**Organize into multi-grade teams.** One grade level builds on the next. You may want to organize teams of teachers by the standard statements or phrases. In other words, a team of mathematics teachers representing all grade levels may work on algebra. Another team may work on geometry, still another on number sense, and another on probability and statistics. Asking teachers to work in multi-grade teams of kindergarten through 12th grade helps to keep gaps in students' knowledge base at a minimum and avoid needless repetition as students move forward level to level.

Multi-grade teams help ensure that students have the proper foundation to succeed at the new higher levels. If, for instance, students are expected to craft a serious essay, present it orally and defend it under examination from peers as a condition of graduation, high school teachers must insist on performance objectives from the time students are able to hold pen and paper. Teachers must nurture student capacity to integrate insight and expression. The word moves through the ranks quickly: High school teachers will get the message out to their elementary colleagues. Get children writing early, regularly and faithfully, every day of every year.

## Insist on Academic Rigor

**Phase out second-class courses.** Most graduates can escape the system having digested only a handful of diluted courses in mathematics, the sciences, and language arts. Few schools have held the line. As performance objective writers correlate or build curricula to standards' specifications, they must ask what "fluff" courses remain on the roster that are not consistent with the new, higher standards. Courses such as functional mathematics, consumer science and occupational preparation are not functional, practical or useful, and have no business appearing in a world-class education lineup.

**Check enrollments in higher-level courses.** For example, algebra and geometry are gateways for high-tech careers and post-secondary study, yet only a few school districts require this course sequence. It may take longer for some, but all students can acquire the knowledge. Somewhere along the way, as a nation, we made a decision that only bright students should go on to study higher-level mathematics and language classes. Innate ability was the linchpin for school success.

## DOSTOYEVSKY COMES TO MAINE

The **Guilford, ME**, school district enrolls 1,000 students in six grade schools, one middle school and one high school. Nearly 10 percent of the students come from neighboring communities and actually pay tuition to attend Piscataquis Community High School; no higher compliment can be paid a public school system. Another relevant fact about the Guilford students: Most are working-class children.

For years the working-class background of the students was behind the "dumbed-down" curriculum at the high school, which included lots of vocational courses with no starch and easy academic courses, suited for kids without much academic talent and little likelihood of going to college. The curriculum was the worst kind of self-fulfilling prophecy: Piscataquis High was in the bottom 10th of Maine high schools.

Then the principal, Norm Higgins, was invited to participate in the creation of

Maine's Common Core of Knowledge, a state-wide effort to identify what all Maine children should know and be able to do to graduate. Energized by this new approach to learning — and challenged in public by one student, who claimed the school's low expectations for him had ruined his career hopes — Higgins decided that the dumbed-down curriculum was unacceptable. To the astonishment of the community (and many teachers), Higgins began to jettison all vocational courses and all easy academic courses. What happened? Set high expectations, get high results. Piscataquis Community High School climbed from the bottom 10th percentile in the state to the top 20 percent in four years.

Today, Piscataquis High also hosts a demanding and spirited seminar on the works of Feodor Dostoyevsky. The brainchild of English teacher Donna Vigue, the seminar is open to any student with the ambition and energy to

take it. How is her class different from similar programs at schools like Deerfield (Deerfield, MA), Peter Stuyvesant (New York, NY) or New Trier (Winnetka, IL)? Piscataquis High is not highly selective — except in what it chooses to teach. Donna Vigue reaches as far as she can and expects her students to do the same.

The fact that they are from one of the poorest parts of Maine does not faze her any more than it does the students (though it did in the beginning). Sitting in on Vigue's class is both sobering and cheering. It's sobering because the work is genuinely demanding. She expects her students to have read the assignment in full and be prepared to discuss it critically and sensitively. And the class is cheering because it is an effective reminder that you get what you set your sights on. Set them low and you get little; set them high and you get what your students deserve.

SPOTLIGHT

**S P O T L I G H T**

## COURSE-TAKING PATTERNS — WHAT GOES ON IN SCHOOLS

School reform literature makes much of the factory model of schooling and our consequent infatuation with measuring what goes "into" schools: dollars, bricks and mortar, books, computers, teachers (and their credentials) and students (including their "background" characteristics). These attributes are important, but they have limited explanatory and predictive power. By the same token, knowing only what comes out the other end, the output of schools, is not enough. Output exists in a context. What goes on in school that makes a difference in the lives of children? What have kids learned as a consequence of going to school? Input only partially explains output.

The missing piece is content, and the most important part of content is what students study. The best available proxy for what they study is course-taking patterns (and to a lesser extent, the tests they take).

Some encouraging trends have emerged over the past decade. Between 1983 (when

*A Nation at Risk* was released) and 1994, the number of students taking the "new basics" or four years of English and three years each of social studies, science and mathematics increased threefold. (*__The Condition of Education 1996__*, Indicator 28)

However, few of our young people graduate from academic programs as rigorous as those abroad. Noted authority **Paul Gagnon**, writing in the *Atlantic Monthly*, observes that the number of students who take fully commensurate programs — even excepting the mastery of foreign languages — would be about one-quarter that of our competition. The standards of U.S. schools pale in comparison with those of other leading democratic nations. Nearly 50 percent of high school seniors in other countries take advanced exams compared to 7 percent who take our top-of-the-line **Advanced Placement** tests. As Gagnon notes in his article, "To our shame, disadvantaged children have a better chance for an equal and rigorous education, and whatever benefit it may bring, in Paris or

*continued on page 47*

The tide is turning. In matters of schooling as in all other endeavors, effort and hard work count more than ever. That message is making a difference in children's lives. Being uninspired is one thing. That's curable. Being labeled innately unable, on the other hand, may be terminal. Why work harder if *continued from page 46*

Copenhagen than in one of our big cities. They educate the many and we the few."

For years, Gagnon warns, we have been telling ourselves that our education system offers broad opportunity while our competitor nations focus only on the elite, that we do poorly because we test everyone, while other countries test only their top students. The truth is that our current system only challenges a minority of students and consigns the rest to less than the best. American education determines from above and in advance that most young people cannot handle, have no interest in and do not need the same content skills and knowledge required of those who are expected to lead our nation. Students are sorted out as early as first grade and consigned to separate tracks for high-ability, average and low-ability students. The all-too-constant correlation between low economic status and low academic placement shows that something more than innate talent is determining the results.

If other countries can challenge all students, so can we. As a nation, this means setting rigorous academic standards for all students and exposing all students to a similar course of study, whether or not they are going to college. In fact, one can argue that high standards are more important for young people who do *not* expect to go to college.

Some people argue that raising academic standards and expectations is elitist, because only the brightest children can reach higher targets. But which system is more elitist: one that expects high achievement from only a small group of students or one that expects it of most? Others fear that the adoption of rigorous standards might further disadvantage our most vulnerable children. But low standards do more damage to children than high ones ever could. Today's practices — different curricula for different students and virtually automatic promotion by age and grade — perpetuate a cruel hoax on both students and society. Sooner or later all young people enter the real world. Those unfortunate enough to have been dumped into lower tracks — systems characterized by unchallenging courses and the accumulation of low-level skills — find themselves wholly unprepared for either post-secondary education or meaningful work.

success is not related to effort? This applies equally to the high fliers. "Simply rely on your talents. Breeze through" is the message. Providing all children with challenging courses is a tall order, but the imperative is clear. There is no time to waste.

## LESSONS LEARNED FROM AN EARLY EFFORT

One of John Murphy's first acts as superintendent in **Charlotte-Mecklenburg, NC**, in 1991 was to assemble 10 of the nation's leading educators to serve on a World Class Schools Panel to sculpt a concrete plan of action for school reform. The panel consisted of such luminaries as former U.S. Education Secretary William Bennett; former U.S. Commissioner of Education Ernest Boyer; Yale University Professor James Comer; education consultant Denis Doyle; former Dean of the Harvard School of Education Patricia Graham; head of the **National Board for Professional Teaching Standards** James A. Kelly; former President of Radcliffe College Matina Horner; John M. Olin Fellow at the Hudson Institute and President of the Thomas B. Fordham Foundation Chester E. Finn, Jr.; Occidental College President John Brooks Slaughter; and College Board President Donald Stewart.

They held divergent views about what change would involve. Each knew of the others by reputation and several knew each other, but the group had never been assembled at one time. They met three times – each time an extraordinary day and a half – to establish the framework for lasting reform. Astonishing even themselves, they reached virtual unanimity on a 14-point document. The panel's deliberations and conclusions can be captured in a single sentence: We must raise standards, then vary the means – not the ends – of education in ways that respect the particular differences among children.

Within days, to put bite into the World Class Schools Panel's final plan, Murphy turned to Susan Pimentel (who had provided meeting continuity, both intellectual and logistical, and had penned the final report) and asked her to draft an initial set of academic standards as a starting point for the community. True to form, he wanted the draft on his desk in 45 days. Pimentel summoned standards documents from as many national and international sources as she could find.

Determined to give the community a real say-so over the standards, Murphy showcased the initial draft at a 2,000-person summit sponsored by *The Charlotte Observer* and the Chamber of Commerce. People gave their initial responses, but it was clear they needed more than a couple of hours. Who should review and work in depth on the draft standards? (Teachers, for starters, as they deliver the standards.) Was the material in the right grades? Did the progression of concepts and skills make sense? Were any topics missing?

Was anyone else needed to review the draft standards? "Yes," concurred Murphy, Pimentel and others. University personnel who were well versed in the college entrance requirements and business people who knew the modern demands of the workplace should weigh in with their thoughts and concerns. Finally, the end-users of standards, namely parents and students, were added to the mix. One year later, Charlotte had a set of school- and community-owned standards that all could be proud of.

# THE TRUTH WILL SET YOU FREE

## Conducting an Academic Analysis

*Setting* high academic standards requires schools and communities to focus on the future: What should students know and be able to do at some future points in time? *Reaching* high academic standards requires schools to take stock of where they stand academically *now*, so they can map strategies to move forward and measure their progress along the way.

### WHAT IS AN ACADEMIC ANALYSIS AND WHY IS IT IMPORTANT?

Taking stock by conducting an academic analysis will help schools and school districts *fine-tune academic policy and significantly improve academic practice.*

Consider an apparently simple set of questions: "How many girls are taking algebra? In eighth grade? In ninth grade? How many of them are eligible for free and reduced-price lunch? How do their test scores compare with those of other girls, in other classes, in other schools in the district, by race and ethnicity? With boys' test scores? What course-taking sequence preceded their enrollment in algebra?" Questions of this kind are not idle ones: The sequence of algebra and geometry, for example, predicts college attendance. Youngsters who take this sequence — black and white, north and south, east and west, Anglo and Hispanic — are equally likely to attend college, according to the Educational Testing Service. Moreover, solid answers to these questions are critically important for both *policy* and *practice*.

If a district understands, for example, that just 15 percent of ninth-grade girls eligible for free lunch take algebra, and 50 percent of these do not pass, it can take steps to improve the success rate of this group of students. It can examine its course-taking policies and offer students more demanding mathematics classes to prepare them for algebra. It can require guidance counselors to steer more students into algebra classes. It can provide teachers instructional assistance and support students with tutoring. All of these actions can help a district improve its bottom line: academic achievement.

### AT A GLANCE

- What is an academic analysis and why is it important?

- Pull the data together and then pull it apart

- Use data to inform and make decisions to improve learning

Most school districts now have the data to answer tough questions (or can get it). Yet few districts raise questions like these — even though they lie at the very heart of the school's mission. There are several reasons for this:

- **History.** Analyzing the academic performance of American schools is almost unprecedented, so pressure for it is lacking. Now, though, local, state and national policy makers and the public are clamoring to know what's going on in schools and why so many graduates lack even basic knowledge and skills.

- **Capacity.** Until very recently, schools did not have the ability to collect, store and manage large data sets. They did not have the people, software or hardware. The advent of new technology, however, has made it possible to collect and analyze incredible amounts of data in very sophisticated ways — and present the analysis in graphic and compelling formats.

- **Culture.** The culture of most American schools has not been disposed to measure *results*. Most of what we have measured over time is *inputs*, or *resources* — dollars, bricks and mortar, books. Today, though, people are focused like never before on results. They no longer assume naively that a sensible mix of inputs leads to desirable results.

Schools themselves now must take the lead in determining what the academic outcomes, or "value-added," of schooling are. They must be able to answer with confidence the question: "In what ways is a student's life improved by having gone to school?" The challenge before the nation's schools is to begin to ask tough questions about academic performance, systematically and regularly. We are convinced that schools must do this themselves, first at the local level, then at higher levels (district and state). The analysis of school performance, like the setting of academic standards, cannot be parachuted in from on high; it must begin at home so that schools can begin to *benchmark* their performance.

In the nation's most successful firms, benchmarking is not something someone does to them; it is something they do to themselves. Firms like AT&T (now Lucent Technologies), which pioneered benchmarking, and Xerox, which refined it, use the practice to understand how effectively processes and relationships are working. Benchmarking is a self-imposed measurement system designed to identify strengths and weaknesses — not to embarrass or finger-point, but to improve performance and profitability. Even successful

*For more about assessments, see Step 5.*

*For more about school and district accountability, see Step 6.*

nonprofit organizations, such as the Museum of Modern Art and the Girl Scouts of America (which management expert Peter Drucker cites as a superbly run organization), ask similar questions: What is our "business" and where do we want to be in the future? How well are we meeting our goals? How do we measure success? What practices must we change to improve our performance?

An academic analysis is the education counterpart of the business "quality process." Schools should approach benchmarking in the same way. Taking stock of academic performance must be supported by the institution as a way to reach higher achievement levels. Three imperatives should guide the practice:

WHAT PRACTICES MUST WE CHANGE TO IMPROVE OUR PERFORMANCE?

- Use data to improve teaching and learning, highlight successes and turn problems into opportunities — *not* to point the finger of blame.

- Keep the public informed with jargon-free reports that are useful to teachers, students, parents, school board members and the community. The messages may be derived from a large, complex, relational database managed by modern computing power, but they should be crystal clear to the general public.

- Continue to update the academic analysis with regular checkups. The metaphor of choice for an academic analysis is medical: diagnose, prescribe, treat, monitor. The process is deliberately circular, designed to support and reinforce the healthy as well as identify those who need special treatment. (We all need special treatment at one time or another; the more we anticipate future needs, the better.)

The academic analysis quantifies, measures and relates the three major dimensions of the school process: resources, context and results (or, to use the language of economics and computers, *inputs, throughputs* and *outputs*):

- Inputs are the *resources* that go into the school: students, teachers, dollars, buildings, books, computers.

- Throughputs are the *context*, the teaching and learning elements that are unique to the school: curricula, syllabi, student activities (for-credit and extracurricular) and classes (such as **Advanced Placement**).

- Outputs are *results*, quantifiable measures of how students are doing or have done: grades; standards- (or criterion-) and norm-referenced test scores (Comprehensive Test of Basic Skills, Scholastic Assessment Test, Advanced Placement); portfolios and other kinds of "authentic" assessments; absenteeism and truancy.

## GETTING THE BOARD ON BOARD

No actors in the system are more important than the members of the school board — if they are on board, anything is possible. If they are fractious or suspicious, there may be no end of trouble. They must believe in an academic analysis, as a means both to improve academic performance and to increase public support for the schools. Indeed, an effective academic analysis capacity is the best thing that can happen to a school board: It provides the information the board needs to frame effective policies. Such information can give the board the confidence to abandon micromanagement. And by providing accurate, timely and useful information, analysis is a bridge to lasting public confidence in the board and its policies.

### AMONG THE MANY BLESSINGS OF PERFORMANCE-DRIVEN SCHOOLS

School boards across the country can barely resist the impulse to micromanage. The impulse is understandable; the members care about the health of their schools, and they have very few tools in their policy kit to intervene effectively. But as management expert Peter Drucker notes, the consequences are usually unacceptable. Members want to interfere in such sensitive areas as personnel, student assignments and textbook selection.

In this regard, the experience of **Beaufort County, SC**, is promising. As standards have moved into the foreground over the past three years, micromanagement has moved into the background. The board is more restrained because it can be. Members know what's going on and can correct course by policy changes; they no longer feel compelled to make discrete administrative interventions. And what's good for the board is good for teachers and principals; even the untutored observer can see the difference at a typical Beaufort board meeting. Board members, teachers and presenters all talk the language of standards. The district's culture has changed.

Done well, the academic analysis serves the needs of everyone in the community. School leaders can make decisions that better serve the academic needs of students. Citizens can judge the effectiveness of schools and policy makers. And when it is up and running in electronic form — as it should be to be most useful — the academic analysis should be easily accessible to everyone, no farther away than the nearest modem.

## Answering Academic Questions

Conceptually, "taking stock," or conducting an "academic analysis," is the academic and intellectual extension of two related activities most schools already perform: *fidelity audits* and *management audits*.

Almost all institutions, public and private, conduct annual fidelity audits to track spending and see that their funds are spent appropriately. Such audits typically are required by law to satisfy administrators, board members, other public officials, parents and citizens that schools are using their funds as intended. The limitation of a fidelity audit is that it shows where money has gone, *not where money should go*. Where the money should go is a matter of policy.

Management audits are a logical extension of fidelity audits. Rather than simply tracking funds, they examine management practices to assess procedural efficiency and effectiveness. By providing clear details of management practices, they help administrators make better decisions. Management audits respond to questions such as these: "Are the cafeteria, crossing guard

## IN BEAUFORT

## ANALYTIC CAPACITY — HOMEGROWN

The **Beaufort County, SC**, school district is typical of many in the United States: It has nearly 15,000 students, spends $5,000 a year per pupil and has an annual budget of $75 million. That's a lot of money, and it means two things: First, such a district can afford to pay for the analytic capacity it needs to solve problems and seize opportunities. Second, it can't afford not to.

The stakes are just too high. No corporation, for-profit or nonprofit, with revenues and expenditures in that range would dare to leave itself unexamined.

To do so invites disaster. Yet few schools analyze their performances. Why? Because they are not expected to. That's why the Beaufort example is so potent. The district bit the bullet.

Beaufort has a small but powerful analysis staff in residence, ready to answer questions from the board, the superintendent and faculty. What is unique about Beaufort's approach is the people. The lead analyst, Catherine McCaslin, has a Ph.D. from UCLA in medical sociology; she came to education by accident. But the accident

turned out to be a blessing in disguise: Not being an educator, she approached the field with a clean slate and only one preconception — school quality makes a difference in measurable ways.

Another part of the Beaufort story is instructive. Even after McCaslin was hired, her talents and capacities were not fully used. Few people in the district knew how much a trained analyst with the right backup and equipment could do on a small budget.

## IN$ITE™: THE FINANCE ANALYSIS MODEL FOR EDUCATION™

While it may not be widely known outside schools, most K–12 general ledger systems used for financial accounting have been designed around regulatory reporting. The accounting is organized around "object" codes that specify what an expenditure is for (such as bus driver, cafeteria or special education). Administrative departments use multiple information systems to collect accounting and student records. This data overload has burdened many school decision makers with more data than they can use — and buried much of the data that would clarify choices. Few schools or districts can tell you where their budget dollars are actually spent.

That's why the international accounting and consulting firm Coopers & Lybrand L.L.P., in cooperation with the U.S. Chamber of Commerce, developed a mission-based management information system specifically for education. Released in late 1996, **In$ite** is a software program that operates on a standard personal computer. It relates a district's expenditures to its practices at both the district and school level. In$ite is not an accounting or general ledger

system — it is a management information software package that converts information from an existing, two-dimensional, "flat-file" financial system (like a general ledger) into a state-of-the-art, multi-dimensional, relational database system, and it uses a common financial language.

Some states such as South Carolina and Georgia have adopted In$ite as a statewide tool for accountability; some districts are implementing it on their own. Those districts now can see how much of their budgets goes to instruction, how much to administration and so on. It does this without the high cost of a system conversion.

In$ite provides over 270 preformatted reports to assist schools and districts in analyzing their information. Even so, the program does not reveal where the money should go. It is policy neutral.

The thinking behind In$ite fueled ruminations about a similar product for an academic analysis dubbed FORESITE™: If we can disaggregate costs and tie that to student achievement, won't we be able to spend scarce dollars more wisely?

and school bus staffs adequate? Are benefit packages competitively priced? Is invoicing and inventory control adequate? Is work flow rational? Is supervision adequate?" Yet no matter how good they are, management audits have the same basic limitation as fidelity audits: They are useful in identifying where human resources are allocated, but they cannot identify where resources *should* be allocated. That, too, is a matter of policy. Fidelity and management audits can determine whether policy is being pursued faithfully, not what policies to pursue.

Neither fidelity nor management audits can tell a district *where to place its academic bets*. Indeed, *bet* is the right word. Most schools rely on intuition and educated guesses to decide where to place academic emphasis. That is why in today's schools having a gifted superintendent and expert principals and teachers is so important. But large institutions cannot run effectively if they must rely on gifted people alone for success; simply not enough of them exist. As management expert Peter Drucker notes, education requires ordinary people to do extraordinary things. The organization whose head is "irreplaceable" is an organization in trouble. Schools are no exception.

Rather than management geniuses, schools need *tools* that are easy to use, clear and precise. Ironically, most schools do not have the sophisticated tools they need to achieve their central mission. An academic analysis serves that purpose. Properly designed and implemented, an academic analysis helps school leaders decide where to invest intellectual and financial resources. A solid academic analysis answers the questions that neither the fidelity nor the management audit can. And it answers questions more convincingly and authoritatively than intuition or best guesses.

## Using Data to Solve Academic Problems

As educators across the nation know, schools use data regularly for many purposes. But schools and school districts rarely have the knowledge and temperament to use education data to either highlight academic success or spotlight problems. Indeed, most districts shy away from using data except in obvious (and often required) ways: counting student enrollment for state financial aid purposes, assembling numbers for required federal or state reports, keeping books of account to satisfy financial audits.

To be sure, these tasks are both useful and important. But too often these tasks consume schools in "administrivia." Schools need to get beyond the overwhelming distractions about the nickels and dimes of budgeting, the detail of scheduling, the blare of the loudspeaker, the chaos of halls and playgrounds, and the micromanagement of the system if they are to succeed. *The school's first order of business is academics.* Everything else should serve that purpose.

AN ACADEMIC ANALYSIS HELPS SCHOOL LEADERS DECIDE WHERE TO INVEST INTELLECTUAL AND FINANCIAL RESOURCES.

AN ACADEMIC
ANALYSIS
SHOULD
INCREASE A
DISTRICT'S
CAPACITY TO
RESPOND
QUICKLY TO
THE NEEDS OF
STUDENTS AND
TEACHERS.

For many schools, however, education data — particularly test score data — has an ominous ring. Teachers, principals, even board members associate published test score data with public criticism. Unfortunately, education data has been used that way in the past and will, no doubt, be used that way in the future. But the only way to counteract the improper use of data is with proper use. Fight fire with fire. Indeed, an academic analysis is designed to go beyond narrow, even pernicious uses of data. Board members, principals, teachers and the community must begin to understand the benefits that sophisticated data analysis offers modern "managers of instruction."

## PULL THE DATA TOGETHER AND THEN PULL IT APART

In assembling academic data for analysis, first conduct a *data inventory*. Chart all the data available using a simple matrix to indicate what is there and what shape it's in. Consider data in terms of its utility: Why is it collected? Data must be useful to teachers, students, administrators, board members and the community to judge programs and policies. If it has no purpose, it should not be collected; to do so simply wastes time, energy and money.

Consider data also in terms of quality. It's important to get it right the first time to establish trust in the community. Moreover, decisions prompted by the academic analysis can be only as good as the data upon which they are based.

The next step is to use a *needs assessment* to identify what else you need to know. Add to your matrix any data categories you'd like to have but don't. You now have a *data inventory* and *needs assessment* in one place. At least initially, you must use available measures, and you may have to limit your academic analysis to 10 or 20 essential categories. But don't stop there — you must continually assess and update your data's program and policy relevance.

The first time you use an academic analysis it helps answer the question, "How are we doing today?" That's a step in the right direction. The bigger issue, of course, is improvement over time, which is why it is important to use it year after year. Schools may then answer the questions, "Are we meeting our academic goals today? What must we do to meet them next year and the year after that? Are the trends positive?" Continuous improvement, as successful companies have learned, is the key to organizational vitality.

By way of comparison, if the academic diagnostic tools are weak, imprecise or inappropriate, the academic analysis will, at the very least, be weak, even useless; indeed, done wrong, the academic analysis may send the district in the wrong direction.

## Disaggregate the Data

At this point, we must stress the importance of disaggregating academic data to the student, classroom and school building level. Aggregate data — or data that's lumped together using averages — should be used where appropriate. But to understand what is going on in schools, the analysis must go below the surface. By way of illustration, "average" data tells you that a lightly dressed camper standing in a strong wind on a freezing cold night in front of a hot camp fire is, on average, comfortably warm.

Only in particular cases are averages useful. Reporting average test scores for entire school buildings by subject is not enough. Average test scores by grade level *and* by subject are another matter. They can be helpful.

Double averaging, on the other hand, where you take the average score of all students in a given grade and then average them to generate a single score for the entire school causes distortions and can mask the impact of lower test scores in one grade or another. (Tests at each grade have their own norms and norming populations, and the number of students at each grade is not equal.) Reporting on progress of some performance measures, while ignoring others, is not sufficient. You need to be able to create both snapshots and trend lines over time. You also need to be able to create comparisons — between classes in your own schools, between grade levels, between schools in your district, between districts in your state and between states.

Beyond test data, you should collect grade information — which includes grade point averages, grade distributions, the number of demanding courses offered (**Advanced Placement** or equivalent) both by subject matter and enrollment, and the number of easy courses — all available by student distributions (including the percent of students prepared to advance to the next grade, percent of students ready for school and upward movement in elementary reading groups).

For example, you should be able to determine almost instantly the number of girls and boys enrolled in **Advanced Placement** mathematics and science courses; the number of youngsters, by age and race, taking algebra, geometry, physics and level 3–4 foreign language courses; and elementary reading and mathematics scores by school room, school building, age, race and socio-economic status. Similarly, knowing which children are not performing at grade level is critical, particularly if they are identifiable by race and income. Tracking honors, scholarships and awards also is instructive.

A well-conceived academic analysis pinpoints academic strengths and weaknesses using a wide variety of useful categories — by student (and by type: age, gender, race, socio-economic status), by grade (or other formal grouping), by school building and by district. It uses test scores, course-taking patterns and indicators of behavior — absenteeism and truancy, for example — to track and identify a student's academic path and trajectory. It helps to

## THE CASE FOR DISAGGREGATED DATA

The **Beaufort County, SC**, schools, like schools across the nation, regularly had reported test score data on an aggregate basis – by school, by grade and by district. Such information is useful in describing how the district compares to other districts, at least in general. But data reported this way has little utility for either policy formulation or improvement of practice; it does not permit analysts, board members or teachers to pinpoint problems or opportunities, successes or failures. Data must be disaggregated in a way that makes it useful – by school, by grade, by race and by socio-economic status, such as eligibility for free and reduced-price lunch.

Until Beaufort presented data this way, conventional wisdom held that the most important variable in student performance was socio-economic status. The intervention strategy this suggested was heterogeneous grouping, putting children of different achievement levels together in the same class. This approach has one virtue: It eliminates "tracking," an approach in which all "slow" kids are put together in one group, "fast" kids in another. A thorough academic audit by analysts Jeff Schiller and Dan Saltrick, then assistant superintendents in **Charlotte-Mecklenburg, NC**, revealed that in 19 of the 26 classrooms examined, the most important variable was not socio-economic status

but race. Black children from all socio-economic sectors were falling far behind. Heterogeneous grouping was making things worse.

The Beaufort schools responded to this data-driven revelation by instituting flexible grouping by achievement levels, not tracking. The change gives more "time on task" to those kids who need it. As they advance they change achievement groups, just the way college students move from French 1 to French 2. Kids who are falling behind need special help – it's that simple. With the right questions ("Who is doing well? Who is doing poorly?"), schools can identify the right "intervention" to correct the problem.

identify instructional practices and policies that inhibit reform. It also permits comparisons — among schools, districts, states and eventually, we hope, countries.

> ➤ **Suggestions on what kinds of data you should collect**

> ➤ **Questions that will help you conduct an inventory of your capacity for collecting, storing and managing data**

## No Quick Fix

By this point, the capacity for conducting an academic analysis may sound both ponderous and expensive. This need not be. To the contrary, a "ponderous" process serves no one's interests. Instead, an academic analysis should increase a district's capacity to respond quickly to the needs of students and teachers.

Is there an "academic analysis" template or software program that a school or district can buy? Is there a "quick fix"? Can someone push a few computer keys and produce a finished report or reports that might be called an academic analysis? The short answer is "not yet." But existing commercial products can deliver elements of this concept. One suite of products, ClassACT from Fox River Learning, will soon use the same database structure for managing school- and student-level data as Coopers & Lybrand's **In$ite**™. Bob Peterson and Dorge Huang have developed a proprietary product called C4Si, permitting high-speed analytic activity from their data "warehouse." Others are sure to follow.

No matter what happens on the software front, however, two conditions must be satisfied. Schools must have the *will* to conduct an academic analysis and the *discernment* to ask the right questions. Sophisticated software will make the job easier and faster, but we know enough to proceed right now. Places like **Beaufort County, SC**, and **Charlotte-Mecklenburg, NC**, have. Our goal in this short book is to provide enough guidance for schools to shape the process themselves.

A district with tough-minded board members and a superintendent with a taste for analysis (and modest human and financial resources) in a community

AN ACADEMIC
ANALYSIS
IS NOT A
ONE-SHOT
ENTERPRISE;
IT IS
CONTINUAL.

that cares about school quality can make significant progress now. In part this is because of the enormous computing power now available at low cost to help problem solvers. The biggest barrier to conducting an effective academic analysis is not lack of technology or money but lethargy and complacency.

## What You Need to Begin

Commitment, commitment, commitment! Take the plunge. Remember that business consultant Philip B. Crosby's book is right, not just for private, for-profit firms: *Quality Is Free!* It is always cheaper to do it right the first time; remediation is a sign of organizational failure. Doing it right the first time not only gives you a competitive leg up, but it also frees downstream resources for additional, high "value-added" activities. The school that understands this knows that a careful academic analysis is not a cost but an investment, one that pays handsomely. It permits you to improve as you go.

Many districts already have competent staffs and simply need to redeploy human resources. But all districts should remember that, while an academic analysis capacity is not expensive, it cannot be conducted on the cheap either. You can beg and borrow staff members from hither and yon to begin, but early on the project must be led by a senior staff person who enjoys the confidence of the superintendent, board and colleagues and who is prepared to stay the course. This person will need a modest support staff. An academic analysis is not a one-shot enterprise; it is continual, precisely as financial audits, teacher training or board elections are continual.

## The Data Maze

In most districts, data is organized functionally and stored where the function is performed. In this connection, remember that schools are like city–states. They feed and transport children, provide health services, maintain major payrolls (often as the biggest single employer in the community), acquire goods and services in large numbers and maintain large and extensive physical plants. Even small school districts have literally millions of "data points" that must be stored somewhere.

Typically, then, school data is stored all over the place. Payroll data is in payroll, food service and transportation data is in administration, teacher data in personnel, student records in pupil personnel services, student test data in other student files, physical plant data somewhere else. Data about curriculum, textbooks and counseling, invoicing, inventory control and acquisitions is in other places. Most significant academic data — and the teacher and student demographic data related to academic performance — frequently is stored in other parts of the organization.

Even as modern data storage capacity began to develop, few schools thought about creating a data warehouse, a common storage place and format. A *data warehouse* is essential for careful analysis, however, because it permits data to be linked electronically. For the analyst, a data warehouse becomes a *data "where house,"* because with effort and imagination it becomes a *relational database.* (Without getting unduly detailed, a data warehouse can be real or virtual; that is, all the data in a district actually can be loaded into one central server or it can be coded to permit a remote analyst to "pull" it up for examination on an "as-needed" basis from a variety of locations. A single server is vastly more efficient, but its absence is not an insurmountable barrier to good analysis.)

A relational database permits analysts to examine all the variables in a system as they relate to each other. Analysts can find out what is working and what is not. For example, they can look at a wide variety of interconnected variables over time, such as:

- student and teacher demographics
- test scores
- grades
- attendance
- discipline

The only limitation is the available data. Some districts will have useful information about their graduates, not just enrolled students: how many by relevant category go on to college (two- and four-year), the military and the workplace. Such data is a potential gold mine for the thoughtful analyst who is concerned with the long-term effects of schooling. But few schools keep such data.

## FORESITE™: An Integrative Data Model

Taking an "education audit" is one thing; knowing what to do with all the information is quite another. After all, American schools have never lacked information: It comes pouring out — attendance data; student test data; and data by school, by classroom, by teacher and on teachers, by district, by state and recently, by nation. The problem is not having too little information; it's having too much, from too many different sources, of varying quality and comparability, and not always having a strategy for using it. The need, then, is for tools for schools that help to make data gathering, analysis and reporting simple and clear to all.

If standards are to be raised and maintained, and if teachers, administrators, parents and community leaders are to take concerted action, these decision makers need to make sense of what all the data means. Whatever the abundance and limits of the education data are, the available information should be woven into a single system or tapestry — an awesome task. But we envision a new data environment, one that is interactive, shared, transparent and useful. In fact, we believe that the following school management information system will eventually appear as a software product that we have christened FORESITE™. Perhaps the easiest way to visualize what such an integrated data system might look like is to examine the following six figures:

**1. Data by Source:** The first step, as shown in **Figure 1**, is to determine the level of information gathered and assembled. This step is critical since information is generated at different points in school systems — from students through teachers, grade levels, schools, type of schools and districts. This data can then be fed "upward" and collected (aggregated) at the central office, and then shared "downward" to principals, teachers, parents and students. **Figure 1** presents a series of six "stair steps" from student to district, disaggregated so decision makers and concerned publics can see how each student, teacher (classroom), grade, school, education level (elementary, middle and high school) and district is performing.

Thus, this first model is traditional, in the sense that districts "roll up" data from the student to the system. The limitation of this rather "flat" model is that typically little effort is made to interrelate the various "buckets" of data. Each successive tier or level simply gathers the information from the preceding tier. Data gathered and reported this way is the simplest, most conventional means to build a database, which permits users to understand what is available. While this format is widely used, useful and necessary, it is only a first step. It is not sufficient for interrelating data levels to school and pupil standards and performance.

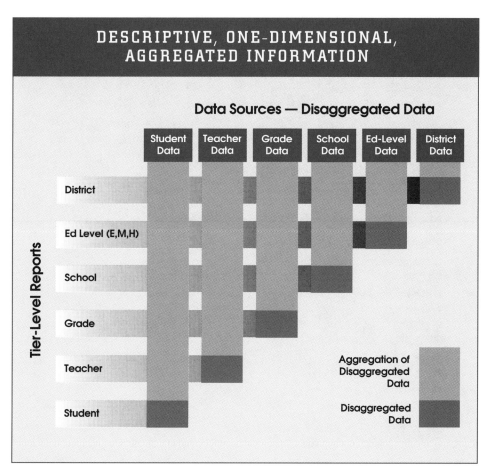

**DESCRIPTIVE, ONE-DIMENSIONAL, AGGREGATED INFORMATION**

Data Sources — Disaggregated Data

Student Data | Teacher Data | Grade Data | School Data | Ed-Level Data | District Data

Tier-Level Reports

District
Ed Level (E,M,H)
School
Grade
Teacher
Student

Aggregation of Disaggregated Data

Disaggregated Data

FIGURE 1

**2. Filling the Buckets:** The next step, then, is to elaborate and define the information necessary to inform and enhance teaching and learning. This format represents a bridge between concept and technique: The boxes start to define the architecture of a relational database. **Figures 2** and **3** fill in the data sets and anticipate the questions that users undoubtedly will ask. Again, we see the six levels, but under each tier are data sets that explore the meaning of the rubrics and specify the data needed.

**Student data:** Seven different data sets about students are useful. Student demographics, for example, give background on students: their ages, gender, years in the district, and family and economic circumstances. In addition to the basic background data, a school management information system also collects and analyzes student test performance data, including local, regional,

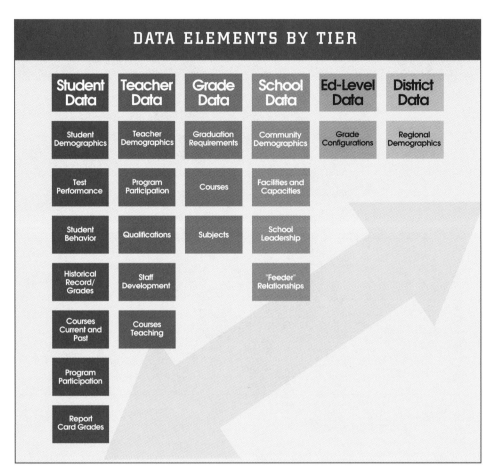

**FIGURE 2**

and state test and appraisal scores; student behavior information such as clubs and extracurricular activities, attendance, truancy and sick days; deportment such as disciplinary action, referrals; and other indicators of success or problems.

Historical records/grades is another useful set of student data that includes transcripts showing work and assessments for at least the last three years and ideally for the student's entire school experience. Data on courses gives a sense of the academic work that students have had and how well they have done. This data is critical to any effort to upgrade the curriculum and improve teaching and learning. Program participation and report card grades are the culmination of the work students have done and what was reported to the family or guardians. Together, these seven types of information on students equip schools and families to figure out what students have done in school and what the "official" record is for all students.

**Teacher data:** Just as they do for students, school systems also need and collect information on teachers: their demographic data, including professional background, training and certification, graduate work, interests and activities. The "personnel database" of the district is likely to have some of this data, but additional information may be needed for decision makers to determine how best to use the talents and skills of professionals at all levels.

Furthermore, as data is "rolled up," the teacher and thus the classroom become the key "teacher-and-learning" unit in the system, and being able to aggregate student information by teacher and subject is crucial. Other teacher data sets include the program participation of teachers, their qualifications and skills, their participation and performance in staff development, and courses taught.

When all the teacher information is available and analyzed, a portrait of the talent and abilities of the teaching force emerges — along with areas where training is needed. For example, if few teachers are qualified in using technology and the Internet in the classroom, the district can ask teachers to participate in workshops. Or if large numbers of teachers are teaching "out of license," the district can take steps to bring in trained, licensed mathematics teachers to teach algebra, physicists to teach physics or musicians to teach music, or it can help teachers take appropriate courses.

**Grade, school and ed-level data:** Information also is needed for the school itself. First, as **Figure 2** shows, district leaders may want to know something about the community demographics that surround each school, the facilities in each building (such data is often kept by the building management and maintenance department and is not always readily available to or readable by teachers and administrators) and what might be done to improve the environment where teaching and learning occur.

School leadership is crucial, as this book shows. Yet little is reported on the qualities of leaders: their sense of mission, their collaborative styles, their ability to inspire and lead. And school feeder patterns may be useful too, since each level up the grade ladder is greatly affected by student learning in previous grades: Positive and negative qualities accumulate, requiring greater effort to improve the "articulation" of each grade with the next and each school level with those above it. Thus, grade configuration is important. An elementary school can consist of grades pre-K through five, six, seven or eight; a middle or junior high can contain grades five, six, seven, eight or nine, which

SCHOOLS THAT ARE RAISING STANDARDS SHOULD CONSIDER ALL FACTORS, AND A RELATIONAL DATABASE IS THE BEGINNING.

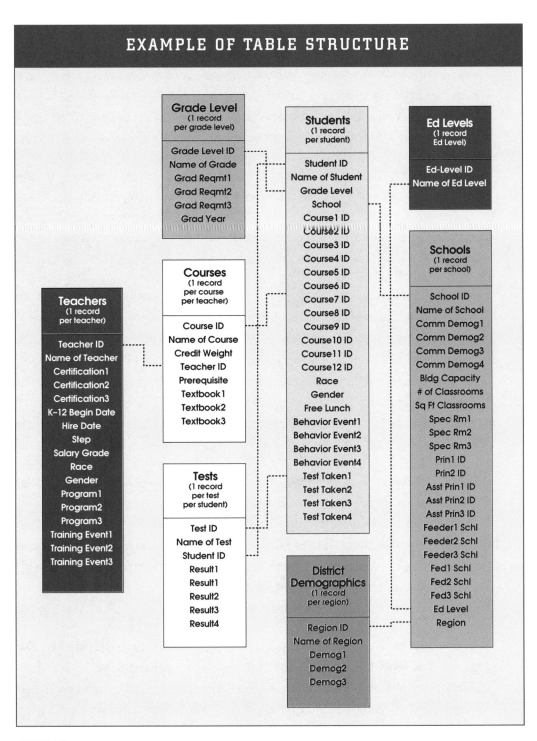

EXAMPLE OF TABLE STRUCTURE

**Grade Level**
(1 record
per grade level)

Grade Level ID
Name of Grade
Grad Reqmt1
Grad Reqmt2
Grad Reqmt3
Grad Year

**Students**
(1 record
per student)

Student ID
Name of Student
Grade Level
School
Course1 ID
Course2 ID
Course3 ID
Course4 ID
Course5 ID
Course6 ID
Course7 ID
Course8 ID
Course9 ID
Course10 ID
Course11 ID
Course12 ID
Race
Gender
Free Lunch
Behavior Event1
Behavior Event2
Behavior Event3
Behavior Event4
Test Taken1
Test Taken2
Test Taken3
Test Taken4

**Ed Levels**
(1 record
Ed Level)

Ed-Level ID
Name of Ed Level

**Courses**
(1 record
per course
per teacher)

Course ID
Name of Course
Credit Weight
Teacher ID
Prerequisite
Textbook1
Textbook2
Textbook3

**Teachers**
(1 record
per teacher)

Teacher ID
Name of Teacher
Certification1
Certification2
Certification3
K–12 Begin Date
Hire Date
Step
Salary Grade
Race
Gender
Program1
Program2
Program3
Training Event1
Training Event2
Training Event3

**Schools**
(1 record
per school)

School ID
Name of School
Comm Demog1
Comm Demog2
Comm Demog3
Comm Demog4
Bldg Capacity
# of Classrooms
Sq Ft Classrooms
Spec Rm1
Spec Rm2
Spec Rm3
Prin1 ID
Prin2 ID
Asst Prin1 ID
Asst Prin2 ID
Asst Prin3 ID
Feeder1 Schl
Feeder2 Schl
Feeder3 Schl
Fed1 Schl
Fed2 Schl
Fed3 Schl
Ed Level
Region

**Tests**
(1 record
per test
per student)

Test ID
Name of Test
Student ID
Result1
Result1
Result2
Result3
Result4

**District
Demographics**
(1 record
per region)

Region ID
Name of Region
Demog1
Demog2
Demog3

FIGURE 3

affects when high school begins. A school management information system takes into account grade configuration and can begin to relate the types of schools as well as the individual schools to the performance of students.

**District data:** Because the district is part of an area of the state, regional demographics have an effect on the schools. Factors such as poverty, dislocation and shutdowns of businesses or military bases all affect the family, the community and thus the school. Schools that are raising standards should consider all the factors, and this relational database is the beginning.

**Figure 3** is a more robust presentation of the previous exhibit. This figure indicates just what may go into the generic "buckets" called teachers, grade level, students, education levels and schools. For example, the teacher file would show the teacher ID number, name, certification, training, hiring date, salary based on step and track, programs and in-service preparation. Grade level is useful, since it explains what each group of students has been taught and what students have learned by that grade. Details might include curricula, textbooks used, teachers involved and how well each student did on courses and programs.

The student record contains the same information for each pupil, including ID, name, grade level, schools attended, courses taken, behaviors and test results. This student data can be seen from a school perspective as well, meaning that data can be linked to other data, building from level to level, school to school. Several states (such as Tennessee) can now track students by their teachers and the performance of their classmates under that teacher.

Once these links are made, we can **connect** student performance — the "value-added" or "gain scores" during a specific time frame (term, semester, marking period, year, years in a school) — to:

- teacher qualifications
- student demographics
- school characteristics
- district qualities
- curriculum
- staff teaching skills

- available resources
- other benchmarks

To refine our opening example, do female students of all races and incomes achieve higher performance in algebra with experienced teachers (trained and licensed in mathematics and with graduate courses in mathematics) than with nonlicensed and/or inexperienced teachers? How do results compare among student types and backgrounds? Do Limited English Proficient (LEP) students learn more English, not to mention mathematics and science, with native speakers?

**3. Answering Multi-Dimensional Questions:** Data is available by student, grade, teacher, school and district. Now what? Data needs to be related and interrelated. And one convenient way to analyze information is to ask pertinent questions, called, in the parlance of the field, "querying the database." **Figure 4** shows what happens when policy makers, parents, teachers and others ask the basic question: How well are our students doing?

This question brings the analysis to the student, focusing on the tests (customized by the district) by poverty, gender, race and summary, and by teacher, grade level and school. And as each "detail metric" is cross-referenced or correlated to other "detail metrics" within different tiers and levels, the number of permutations grows since each single item can be "exploded" into multiple items by relating it to other categories of data. As a value-neutral tool, this approach can be used by teachers to help them adjust to the needs, backgrounds and demands of students and their subjects. School leaders will find it useful in making the appropriate classroom assignments and enhancing their programs, and it helps inform parents as well.

For example, the state of New York recently moved from "minimum competency" assessments to grade-level assessment for all students. Suddenly, parents in upper-class suburbs such as Scarsdale and Irvington in Westchester County and Oyster Bay on Long Island realized that 25 percent and 40 percent of third-grade students, respectively, were not reading on third-grade level — a fact obscured by the minimum competency testing in 1996, which only flagged students reading one or more years below grade level.

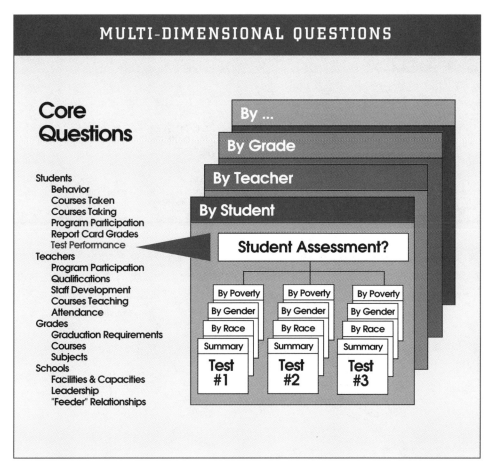

**MULTI-DIMENSIONAL QUESTIONS**

Core Questions

Students
  Behavior
  Courses Taken
  Courses Taking
  Program Participation
  Report Card Grades
  Test Performance
Teachers
  Program Participation
  Qualifications
  Staff Development
  Courses Teaching
  Attendance
Grades
  Graduation Requirements
  Courses
  Subjects
Schools
  Facilities & Capacities
  Leadership
  "Feeder" Relationships

By ...
By Grade
By Teacher
By Student

Student Assessment?

By Poverty | By Poverty | By Poverty
By Gender | By Gender | By Gender
By Race | By Race | By Race
Summary | Summary | Summary
Test #1 | Test #2 | Test #3

FIGURE 4

Parents were upset, and real estate sales people were nervous. Superintendents began holding public meetings to explain the limits of the test. A policy review found that elementary schools prevented teachers from assigning homework for students until third grade and that teachers were not teaching phonics techniques at all. These policies were reconsidered and changed, thanks to data available by student, grade level, teacher, school, subject and policy area. New standards, tests and information transformed the environment and helped districts reconsider programs, policies and pedagogy.

**4. The Dynamics of Data:** **Figures 5** and **6** show the power of data interactions, as information is aggregated by teacher, grade, school and district.

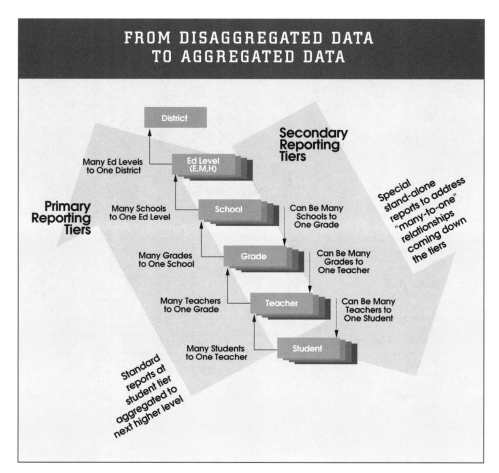

**FROM DISAGGREGATED DATA TO AGGREGATED DATA**

FIGURE 5

**Figure 5** illustrates how aggregation occurs from the bottom to the top of the system, from:

- many students to one teacher
- many teachers to one grade
- many schools to one education level
- many education levels (and schools) to one district

The model has the power to produce special stand-alone reports that address this "many-to-one" relationship. Rather than starting at the top as most reporting systems seem to do, requiring the concerned analyst to "drill down" to get information, a school management information system begins at the bottom and builds upward. Each higher tier contains everything in the lower tiers, permitting both top-down analysis and bottom-up investigation.

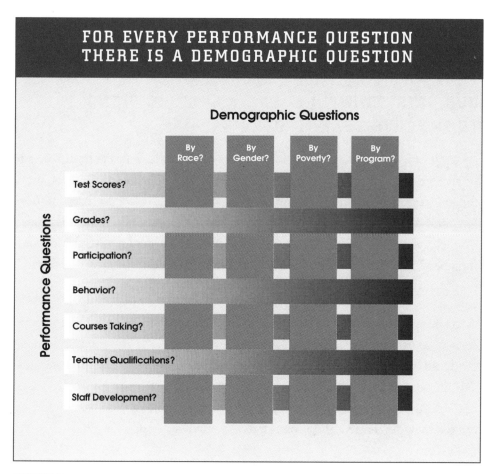

**FOR EVERY PERFORMANCE QUESTION THERE IS A DEMOGRAPHIC QUESTION**

Demographic Questions

By Race? | By Gender? | By Poverty? | By Program?

Performance Questions

Test Scores?
Grades?
Participation?
Behavior?
Courses Taking?
Teacher Qualifications?
Staff Development?

FIGURE 6

**Figure 6** puts the process into a slightly different light. For each performance question, a set of demographic questions is introduced (By Race? By Gender? By Poverty? By Program?). The matrix allows decision makers at all levels to raise key questions about test scores and takes into account relevant concerns about gender, race, socio-economic status and school programs. In this illustration, the focus is student-centered by group and background. The data also can be depicted by teacher, school or grade configuration.

A school management information system then produces reports that accurately identify areas of the greatest weakness and risk to teaching and learning. For example, aggregate test scores may paint a picture of a school district with "moderately high" average scores, but such reporting may obscure the significant number of students (and schools and grade levels) who are not doing well. "Cutting" and presenting data by these categories and levels raise the red flag and allow more carefully calibrated analysis to begin.

## USE DATA TO INFORM AND MAKE DECISIONS TO IMPROVE LEARNING

As academic performance data becomes available, the district should decide what to do with it. The option we recommend is publishing one or more reports about the academic analysis. Several rules govern the presentation. First and foremost are privacy considerations: At no time can the data be used publicly to reveal information about individual students, teachers or staff members. Second, the district has a profound obligation to present data in a way that ordinary people can understand.

Accordingly, reports should be written in clear, expository prose to place the data in a user-friendly context. Whenever appropriate, the data should be rendered graphically. Raw data (the actual numbers, not just percentages) should be available either in the body of the report or as an appendix to reassure more sophisticated readers. Most important, the reports should be handsomely formatted and illustrated, attractive and appealing.

## IN GUILFORD

## USING ACADEMIC DATA TO SPUR EXCELLENCE

In **Guilford, ME**, education turnaround began with cold, hard facts. When Norm Higgins, then principal of Piscataquis Community High School and now district superintendent, started digging around for academic data, he exposed a scandalous lack of achievement. The high school consistently ranked among the bottom 10 of 116

high schools on Maine's state-wide tests in six academic areas; one year, it was dead last. By disaggregating student data, the high school found that the "cream of the crop," the top 20 percent, were doing just fine, but the remaining 80 percent — the have-nots who made up the bulk of the student population — were performing abysmally.

Worse, there was no public outcry, because people rationalized that the have-nots couldn't be expected to do any better. Higgins and a group of five frustrated high school teachers believed differently. And they began to ask themselves, "What would it take to build the best high school in the state?" That's when they started shaking up the school and, later, the school district.

## Who Is the Audience?

Education policy makers (school board members and the superintendent) and practitioners (teachers, principals, deans, coordinators) will be keenly interested in the academic analysis. So will a wider audience, including parents, students, journalists, community and special interest groups, and the general public.

While the academic analysis process must satisfy many audiences, we stress that its one overarching purpose is to lay the groundwork for improved teaching and learning. Use it to tell all who are interested (and pique the interest of those who are not): Where are students academically, in measurable terms? Who is learning what?

---

### NO JARGON

Jargon is either the last refuge of a weak mind or is a deliberate attempt to baffle, bewilder, perplex, bamboozle and confuse the uninformed reader. Report authors should bend over backward to be clear, understandable and focused.

---

## The Keystone Report

Four categories, or tiers, of reports on the academic analysis are important. The keystone document should be an annual *state of the schools* or *condition of education* report prepared by the superintendent and the senior staff for formal presentation to school board members and the larger community.

Each year it should contain comparative core data that illuminate resources, context and results. It should provide comprehensive descriptive information on expenditures, enrollments, demographics, course-taking patterns, grades and test scores. Year-to-year changes of any magnitude, such as a sudden surge in enrollment or a change in state-mandated tests, should be explained and analyzed.

The theme of the report should be how the schools are doing academically; collateral information and analyses should be included as appropriate (discipline and behavior problems, relevant data on extracurricular activities and the like). This keystone document should become embedded in the district culture as the principal tool for communicating. It must be brutally honest. If the community begins to see it as a whitewash, it won't wash.

➤ **A model state of the schools report**

## Special Reports on Policy and Practice

The second-tier reports should be sharply focused *special reports on policy and practice*, data-rich analyses that highlight problems and opportunities. The major audiences for these reports are the people who straddle the fine line between policy and practice: principals, coordinators, master teachers, lead teachers and the like. Among these people, "practice is policy," and both stimulating and satisfying their curiosity about "what works" are critically important. The more they know the better; the more they want to know the better. This is the pivotal audience in any school district; if the superintendent and board are wise, these are the people they listen to. Teachers, particularly new ones, look to them for guidance and inspiration, as do parents and students.

Develop a taste for thoughtful and useful academic analysis among this influential group and the battle for education excellence will be won.

➤ **A model special report on policy and practice**

## Impact on Practice Reports

The third-tier reports are the *impact on practice reports*, designed to serve teachers and principals by responding to issues of central concern to them. Such reports are designed to be immediately useful and whet an appetite for similar work in the future. These reports go after the nitty-gritty issues that a teacher or principal faces in the day-to-day business of schooling. To wit: What happens when Title I kids are exposed to an after-school program rather than a pull-out program? Does English as a Second Language learning improve with native English speakers in the classroom? What is the impact of cross-age tutoring? The list of questions is nearly endless; involving teachers and principals in asking and answering them is a powerful school improvement tool — and it builds community support as well.

➤ **Model impact on practice reports**

## Community-Based Reports

The fourth-tier reports are *community-based reports*, designed to answer questions of particular interest to the community. No reports will be more important to the school's long-term well-being than these. Community-based reports should satisfy legitimate community interest in what schools are doing — or failing to do. The National Association for the Advancement of Colored People, for instance, will want to know about the number of black males in **Advanced Placement** courses; the chamber of commerce will want to know about work readiness; military recruiters will want to know about participation in Reserve Officers Training Corps programs; real estate sales people will want to know about academic performance, school by school. And so on. Not only do community-based reports answer these questions, but they also build community support and demand for excellence.

➤ **Model community-based reports**

## IN CHARLOTTE-MECKLENBURG

# USING DATA TO QUESTION COMFORT ZONES

John Murphy, **Charlotte-Mecklenburg, NC's** former superintendent and extraordinary agent of change, used data to get people out of their comfort zones. Four charts made his point succinctly: Three showed great evaluations for principals, teachers and the central office staffs; the last showed poor student performance. "In other words," Murphy says, "what they were saying is that the adults were doing a great job, this was really the kids' fault. We had to change that mindset or else we weren't going to get anywhere."

Murphy used the charts as something of a litmus test for the central office staff. Administrators who didn't respond constructively with positive approaches to change were out; more than a handful lost their jobs within six months. So convinced was Murphy that student achievement data was the tool for diagnosis, prescription and real school accountability that he dedicated an entire division to its analysis and hired a research expert — Jeff Schiller — to take charge of the effort. Traditionally, diagnoses of education problems were made on the basis of anecdotes and best

guesses. Sometimes they were right; sometimes they were not. With Murphy came regular and thorough academic audits to direct decision-making in Charlotte-Mecklenburg — much of which serves as the basis for this chapter. He acknowledges that taking inventory is politically easier for new superintendents, but he says incumbents also need the courage to face the truth. "They have to be willing to own up to the fact that they made mistakes and that they weren't doing their jobs. Tell the truth. That's the only way to survive."

## Taking the Pledge: Motivation

Few generalizations about education can be uttered with complete confidence, but two can. First, *no district in the nation can become a performance-driven district without a high-quality academic analysis.* Second, *no district in the nation can use an academic analysis effectively without wholesale training,* from the board to the central staff to principals and teachers. Every district in America could profit from effective training in the uses and abuses of education data, including the uses of computers. Disaggregating test data by grade and classroom to more effectively target instruction, group students and monitor progress is critical to improving the capacity of teachers.

The key is motivation. In the case of the academic analysis, every participant in the schooling process must be motivated to develop and use it and be convinced that it is essential. This is most difficult the first time around; once communities see the power of data in revealing academic performance, they clamor for more. District-wide passion for counting, measuring and analyzing builds — not for its own sake, but as the principal tool to improve teaching and learning.

Board members see the utility of academic analysis as they set policy and monitor practice; the superintendent finds the academic analysis useful in overseeing the life of the system; principals and teachers find the academic analysis useful in instructional management and delivery; students, parents and the community find it useful in academic learning and learning about the schools themselves.

Remember the old saw: "Set your goals carefully, because you're almost sure to meet them." A thoughtful academic analysis lets you identify opportunities, set targets and measure the extent to which you meet them.

# SEIZE THE
# DAY

## Reorganizing for Change and Building Staff Capacity

Developing rigorous academic standards and then making them stick will not happen unless schools fundamentally change how they are organized. More power and authority should go to the front lines, to principals and teachers. The central office should take on a new role, as a provider of services that help school staffs do their jobs better. Organizational charts must be turned upside down. No more top-down decision-making. Everyone takes on new roles and responsibilities.

Such an upside-down world requires schools to invest in more professional development, lots of it. For most school districts, this level of investment will be new — but absolutely essential. To help students reach high levels of achievement, school and district staffs will be working in much different ways — with students, with each other and with communities. New behaviors and new skills don't come naturally to most people; they have to be learned.

## FOCUS ON RESULTS, NOT RULES

Regulatory regimes, the norm in American education, hold tightly to a compliance mentality, specifying what school staffs are to do and how they are to do it. The people whose lives are most affected, teachers and principals, are powerless. This world is governed by categories and rules, formulas and guidelines. Under command-and-control administrations, central management is full of people whose only job is to verify whether schools are adhering to the rules.

Legions of highly paid personnel churn out an inexhaustible supply of prose and policy about how to teach. Classroom teachers and students rarely see them. Taxpayers are oblivious to their existence. Yet they have most schools in a stranglehold. Rules govern testing, time, textbooks, curriculum, compensation, credentialing, competence, staff training, attendance and graduation requirements — every facet of schooling. Left unattended they leave little wiggle room for reform. Teaching is truly a profession in only a very few

### AT A GLANCE

- Focus on results, not rules

- Give teachers and principals more control

- Change the orientation of the central office

- Tailor instruction to students

- Use time differently

- Rethink teacher development

- Give principals new leadership and management skills

schools. That's not to say that large numbers of teachers and principals aren't professionals. Many are. But they become so in spite of the system, not because of it. Rules don't teach. If children don't learn, it doesn't much matter that educators follow the regulations and guidelines and spend the public's money according to law. In the long run, districts need to wipe these constraints from the books to reflect the new priorities.

Switching gears to a system that runs on incentives and consequences decentralizes decision-making and allows almost all productive work to take place in classrooms where teachers meet students. Incentive systems specify what is to be achieved and leave it up to those at the school level to decide how. A system where schools are trusted to do the right thing is more efficient than micromanaging schools. Performance-driven schools make reams of regulations and regulators obsolete and send needed people back to the classroom.

Schools must deregulate and then reregulate according to new priorities. Local policies and regulations are key targets, but for lasting success, state

## IN BEAUFORT

## PART-TIMERS

Small schools have special needs. One way to help meet these needs is with a part-time principal, a person who can provide guidance without soaking up scarce resources – a good theory but difficult in practice. But it is in practice in **Beaufort County, SC**, not because of an edict from on high, but because school-site budgeting and management are becoming institutionalized. Port Royal Elementary School with 90 children (it adjoins the part of Port Royal Sound where the storm scene in **Forrest Gump** was filmed) is the second smallest school in Beaufort. (The

smallest is Daufuskie, where **The Water Is Wide** was set. Beaufort is a cinematic and literary moveable feast.)

When the Port Royal principal retired, the school was confronted with a dilemma and an opportunity. It could fill the post with a full-timer and spend more than $60,000 a year on salary and benefits, or it could hire a part-timer (on contract) and get the job done for less than half the price. The balance would revert to the Port Royal account, available to invest in other programs. Could they find someone to fit the bill? They did.

Melissa Shepherd, the energetic principal of **Broad River Elementary School**, was invited by Port Royal to meet with teachers and parents. Was she interested? She sure was. Now in her second year, she continues to give her attention to Broad River and spends a few hours a week at Port Royal. If this solution had been imposed on Port Royal by the central office (and the savings retained by the central office), the faculty and parents would have been outraged. Because it was their solution – and a sensible one – it works.

laws also must give way to more enlightened thinking. That said, the principal constraints to quality schools for all American children live not in our laws and structures, but in our minds and hearts. Those are the barriers we must first eliminate.

➤ **A checklist of new rules for the new world of standards**

School-based management alone will not improve schools, an observation confirmed by recent research. Decisions are not intrinsically "better" because they are made at the school level — unless the system leaders insist, as John Murphy did in **Charlotte-Mecklenburg, NC**, that certain conditions are understood and in place:

- School-based management activities should first and foremost serve the new rigorous academic standards and the mission statement that commits the system to providing an excellent education to all students. School-based management activities should operate against a backdrop of explicit improvement goals for schools and staffs. Before a decision is made, schools must ask how the activity contributes to student and school success.

- Teachers, other staff members and parents should be involved in reviewing current practices and designing new ones. Moving the locus of control to the school site does not mean substituting the principal's decision-making authority for the superintendent's. Without shared decision-making and without support from all sectors, change in the classroom where teachers meet students is likely to be slight.

- Giving power, authority and control over decision-making to people who have no experience with it, little taste for it and high levels of anxiety about it won't work without a serious investment in staff training. Specifically, training must be provided in three key areas: data collection and analysis (how to accurately diagnose problems, best allocate scarce resources, assess the progress of students, and make appropriate instructional modifications); team-building (collaborative decision-making and problem-solving); and technical skills in personnel, financial and record-keeping policies.

- All policies and procedures that function as barriers should be eliminated. School staffs need the authority to use budgets, personnel, time and materials with as few restrictions as possible. Above all else, they need to be given the authority to adapt instructional procedures as they see fit.

*For more on setting standards, see Step 2.*

*For more on accountability, see Step 6.*

- Rather than a "cookie-cutter" approach to site-based management, let schools decide how much they would like to take on. Perhaps a school wants the flexibility to staff the school instructionally but does not care to take on decisions about food or janitorial services. Many schools don't want to manage the facility, they want to manage the instructional program.

➤ **Commissioned papers by New American Schools on transforming school designs**

## GIVE TEACHERS AND PRINCIPALS MORE CONTROL

The keys are innovation, entrepreneurship and autonomy. To produce a system full of creative ferment, teachers and administrators must have a bigger voice, a real stake in school success. They need to "strut their stuff," to challenge the *status quo* and to be held accountable for the ends, not the means, of education.

Under a performance-based system, principals and staffers rise to the head of their organization. They control their own work conditions and no longer

## IN CHARLOTTE-MECKLENBURG

## ACADEMICS AND AN EDIFYING CAFETERIA

At one of Superintendent John Murphy's first site-managed schools in **Charlotte-Mecklenburg, NC**, the principal, Pete Stone, decided to leave two janitorial positions unfilled. The dollar savings went to program enrichment; the work was performed by the students. Stone used the tried-and-true recruitment scheme developed by Tom Sawyer when he whitewashed Aunt Polly's fence: He made working as a student janitor an honor, not a burden, and adult janitors showed them the ropes. (As a special treat, visitors get to vacuum and clean blackboards in front of the assembled students and teachers. We know from firsthand experience.)

Everyone gained: The school had more money, it was cleaner and neater; the kids learned a powerful lesson about stewardship; and the remaining janitors became teachers. Not satisfied with this innovation (copied shamelessly from Japanese schools), Stone hired as head cook a young French-trained chef who offered a dazzling menu of French food in the wilds of southern Mecklenburg County. Knowing he had a real draw, he opened the cafeteria to the community with one proviso: The adults who came to eat had to distribute themselves among the children. No cliques. In one fell swoop, the principal had a happy (and well-fed) tutoring network.

Are these accomplishments John Murphy's or Pete Stone's? Both. Neither could have done any of this alone. Together they worked wonders.

## WITH OWNERSHIP COMES CHANGE

Building on research from corporate America and drawing on the values of a market-driven economy, we know that:

- Those closest to students are in the best position to know what students need and how best to serve them.

- Decisions can be made more quickly at the school level.

- Putting trust in those on the front line makes it more likely the staff will rise to the occasion.

- Authority and accountability go hand in hand. Without authority to make changes, there can be no accountability.

- Freeing the staff has as much to do with increasing productivity as encouraging experimentation and greater diversity.

- When staff members are forced to work together to address problems and improve schooling, a shared sense of ownership develops.

- With ownership comes change.

---

spend their energies trying to beat the system. The switch produces an immediate payoff. Productivity improves. The deck, once stacked against creative and entrepreneurial educators, now favors them.

A key to staff motivation is control over their own professional lives. Bosses can tell workers how to do the job effectively and efficiently, and they may be right. But if workers aren't convinced, the best plans won't be acted on. By transferring control to workers, effectiveness improves, often dramatically. One need only look at corporate leaders such as Motorola, IBM and Xerox.

Given direct access to financing, principals and teachers can design schools that right the current wrongs of education. Holding student outcomes constant, they can tailor-make their schools to fit their particular student population.

## CHANGE THE ORIENTATION OF THE CENTRAL OFFICE

As schoolhouse professionals are given autonomy to do their jobs well — free to organize themselves subject only to the requirement that their students

## SPOTLIGHT

## CHANGES AT HEADQUARTERS

The real sign of change in any organization is change in the central office. If the central office is the same, the rest is window dressing. **Charlotte-Mecklenburg, NC**, at the forefront of the school change movement, saw the most radical transformation. Superintendent John Murphy's formation of leadership teams of principals and elimination of regional superintendents not only sent a strong message, but these actions also reflected major changes in both policy and practice. Most important was his decision to have all 118 principals report directly to him, a revolutionary change in school district management.

**Red Clay, DE**, Superintendent Bob Simons assembles his principals on a weekly basis as a cabinet. They meet to hammer out issues and reach collegial decisions. Simons is still in charge, but he's not a dictator.

The biggest change in the **Beaufort County, SC**, central office is invisible but no less important. Superintendent Herman Gaither does not hold an administration credential. In the jargon of the trade, he is unqualified.

Considered one of the most gifted superintendents in the nation, Gaither is a perfect fit with his performance-driven school district, and his success sends a strong message: Performance is more important than papers.

**Murfreesboro, TN's** biggest change is its school board. Always perfectly competent, the board recently ratcheted its quality even higher by electing exceptionally well-qualified new members, among them a local businessman, two physicians and a professor of art history. The change is noteworthy because of the national lament that getting qualified candidates to stand for board election is harder than ever. Not in Murfreesboro: The excitement of the Extended School Program (ESP) is contagious.

**Guilford, ME's** new superintendent is its old high school principal, Norm Higgins. A member of the National Education Commission on Time and Learning and the Council for Basic Education Board of Directors, Higgins was asked to do for the district what he did in Piscataquis Community High School.

succeed — the central office must loosen the reins. The central office should change its orientation from mandating and prescribing to nurturing and supporting school efforts. In the new regime, central office staffs report to principals. Top-down, memo-driven administration is no longer tolerated. District staffs become "brokers" of needed services rather than regulatory overseers. Authority for decisions that relate direction of instruction are vested at the schoolhouse level.

Instead of allotting the same mix of staff members to all schools, districts give each school an equal number of full-time equivalent staff members and allow schools to determine the precise kind of staff members and expertise they need. Other staffing decisions such as hiring, evaluation and promotion decisions must be school-driven.

In addition, districts should hand over control for school budgets to school staffs, giving them the discretion to buy the services needed, such as textbooks, part-time staff members, instructional materials, curriculum coordination and professional development. Quick and ready access to funds helps to keep the good ideas coming.

If talent and services from the central office don't fit the bill, school staffs then have the resources and freedom to buy from outside contractors. Market pressures mean the central office has to respond to customer demands. No customers, no work. Either the central operation reorganizes to meet the demands, or it goes out of business.

## TAILOR INSTRUCTION TO STUDENTS

The old model of schooling is an "extraction" model: Students are expected to extract whatever they can from the instruction. Children who learn at a different pace or in a different way are out of luck. Struggling students are forced to move with the class, pushed on to the next task before they are ready. Caught in the powerful dynamic of failure, they are penalized with poor grades and pushed into dull classes until they fall hopelessly behind.

As _Prisoners of Time_, the 1994 report of the National Education Commission on Time and Learning, records, the high fliers easily fall into the trap as well. Many become frustrated and indifferent as they are forced to wait for others to catch up. Students who fall somewhere in the middle aren't immune either. They are often overlooked as teachers struggle to motivate the most capable and to assist those in difficulty. People do not learn alike, and to run schools one way with one style is not just prejudicial, it's counterproductive. In the words of educator **E.D. Hirsch**, "Gaps in excellence and fairness explain why the most consistent problems of misbehavior occur among students at the top and bottom of the academic range, one group antagonized by boredom, the other by boredom compounded with humiliation."

"GAPS IN EXCELLENCE AND FAIRNESS EXPLAIN WHY THE MOST CONSISTENT PROBLEMS OF MISBEHAVIOR OCCUR AMONG STUDENTS AT THE TOP AND BOTTOM OF THE ACADEMIC RANGE."

— E.D. Hirsch

As **Guilford, ME**, Superintendent Norm Higgins says, the problem is not that schools are not what they used to be. The problem is that they are *precisely* what they used to be. Little seems to have changed in how schools teach children, even though many of today's students are very different. Due to pressures beyond their control, many students don't come to school equipped with the attitudes, values or energies to cope with classes dominated by teacher lectures, textbooks, short-answer activity sheets and silent work on their own. Exploring new teaching options is incumbent on schools. Once parents and the broader public are certain that the school's aims and expectations are specific, high and equal, they welcome local experimentation and new configurations of teaching.

## Use Different Approaches and Techniques

The way teachers deliver instruction should look and feel different school to school, classroom to classroom, group to group, even child to child. Teachers need to organize learning so that it is tied to specific tasks emphasizing practicality and measurable results.

Teaching students the same amount in the same way at the same rate at the same age defies research, experience and common sense. Individuals grow at different rates — intellectually, physically and emotionally — with unpredictable starts, stops and surges along the way. Most children have fast subjects and slow subjects and days when insight comes more readily. Children do not arrive at school ready to learn at the same pace or in the same manner. The current structure — 13 grades and 25 students to a classroom — is a better way to keep track of students than teach them. The system needs to flex with the student — but not by compromising the curricula or abandoning accountability for staffs to move students forward briskly.

Under a new vision of schooling that pays less attention to the students' age and allows students to advance as they master the material, students at relatively similar levels of accomplishment in a particular subject study together. But virtually *all* students at *all* levels — and this is a critical difference from the "tracking" that goes on today — study the same rich content. No more exemplary curriculum for some students and a watered-down version for the rest. No more smart-kid/dumb-kid curricula to stigmatize children. No more being "sentenced" to a particular group without opportunity for deliverance either. The curricula are the same for all students except the most severely intellectually handicapped. The same rigorous standards that apply to the highest-performing groups apply to all groups. Since the same core material is being covered, students who are ready for faster-paced instruction are able to advance. If students find they are unable to handle the new demands, they can drop back at any time during the school year. Education is available on an as-needed basis, in real time, and tailored to the learners' particular requirements. Students move in and out of performance groupings as they master the material.

Academic knowledge should not be withheld on the "principle" that students "aren't yet ready" for more rigorous study. Students need to be pushed to work hard, and when students are not approaching the standard within expected time frames, they need to be pressed to work harder. The good news is that students themselves want to be challenged much more than they are, a finding confirmed by *Getting By: What American Teenagers Really Think About Their Schools*, from Public Agenda, a New York–based non-profit research organization that specializes in public attitudes about schools.

Expectations need to be clear that staffs will be held accountable for moving students ahead, for the "value-added" of teaching. The best classrooms bring all students along at a steady pace, monitoring success for all at each step, providing compensatory instruction as needed, and giving challenging extra work to talented and eager students.

No more assuming "slow in one area, slow in all areas." Experience clearly demonstrates that once students are assigned to lower-level groups, they stay there, perpetuating a cycle of disappointment and failure. Under a performance-based (as opposed to ability-based) system, a decision to assign a student to a group in one content area is made independently of other content areas. Because a student is assigned to a slower mathematics group doesn't mean he or she can't handle faster-paced work in reading, writing or history.

Even within a content area, more subtle configurations are available. The new system is not about who's smart and who's not — but who knows what and who still needs to learn. As a result, all students who need to learn fractions, for example, study together without regard to how their overall skill levels in mathematics stack up against one another's. At the same time they are studying fractions together, some also may be studying in an algebraic concepts group

**THE NEW SYSTEM IS NOT ABOUT WHO'S SMART ... IT'S ABOUT WHO KNOWS WHAT AND WHO STILL NEEDS TO LEARN.**

while others brush up on the basic operations of multiplication and division. As students move at different paces in different subjects, groups are flexible and short-term.

---

### NEW AMERICAN SCHOOLS

One of the most ambitious efforts to test new school designs for effective learning has been undertaken by **New American Schools**, a consortium funded by major U.S. corporations and foundations. New American Schools used most of its funding to develop eight innovative, "break-the-mold" school systems; the models range from the hands-on learning emphasis of Expeditionary Learning Outward Bound to the back-to-basics, standards-based approach of Modern Red Schoolhouse.

---

### Provide School Choice

Exposing all students to higher-level material, grouping them differentially and pacing them differently set the stage for modifying the delivery of instruction to meet the child. Like adults, some children learn best by doing, others by listening, others by viewing. Harvard researcher **Howard Gardner** asserts that individuals differ in their type of intelligence and learning: linguistic intelligence (a playwright, for example), logical-mathematical intelligence (a scientist), musical intelligence (a composer), spatial intelligence (an airline pilot), body-kinesthetic intelligence (an athlete), interpersonal intelligence (a salesperson) and intrapersonal intelligence (a philosopher). Whether or not you agree with Gardner's theories of multiple intelligences, children clearly differ in interest and aptitude. Schools need to find ways to tap into a child's particular genius and teach to that strength.

We pay a lot of lip service to treating each child individually, but general practice belies the assertion. School assignments made solely on the basis of geography presume children are interchangeable. Choice through academic-specialty schools or classrooms blasts away that misguided assumption. Choice celebrates the differences and uses them to good effect. What better way to capture young people's minds than to enroll them in schools they want to attend, tailored to their particular interests and learning styles? High-performance schools around the country, including New York's LaGuardia

# CHARTERS: OLD WINE IN NEW BOTTLES

Are charter schools simply the latest education reform fad or might they have some staying power? We are convinced they are here to stay, for several reasons. First, they are an old idea with a long track record. Many of the nation's most prominent high schools are, functionally, charter schools. For example, Philadelphia's Central High (also known as Boys High) was created by special legislation in the mid-19th century as a freestanding, publicly funded high school (it is led by a president, not a principal). One hundred fifty years later, it is still a distinguished school (as is its counterpart, Girls High). Peter Stuyvesant, Bronx Science and Brooklyn Tech also enjoy statutory protection. (Without it they would have been absorbed by the regular system long ago. The late Al Shanker of the **American Federation of Teachers** (AFT) was a Stuyvesant alumnus; his successor, Sandra Feldman, is a Bronx Science alumna.) In addition, there is Lowell in San Francisco, Boston Latin, the North Carolina School of Science and Mathematics (created by then-Governor Jim Hunt in 1979) and the Illinois Mathematics and Science Academy (now a decade old).

Second, charter schools already are securing an impressive track record. Early Hudson Institute research by Chester E. Finn, Bruno Manno, Greg Vanourek and Louann A. Bierlein shows high levels of racial integration, significant services for the handicapped, ample socio-economic integration and high levels of teacher satisfaction and parent support.

> **"Charter Schools in Action,"
> a Hudson Institute project**

Third, public opinion polling for the past two and a half decades reveals high levels of public support for schools in small towns and villages — teachers, parents and children all like small school districts and frequently small schools. Small size is an essential element of charter schools. A preference for private schools (especially among minority parents) also is strong; charter schools provide many of the perceived benefits of private schools yet remain in the public sector.

Fourth, and most important, charter schools are exciting places in which to teach, and the teaching profession (including the **National Education Association** and AFT) is increasingly interested in the movement. For a stirring description from a teacher's standpoint, see Sarah Kass' piece, "City on a Hill," in *The Public Interest* (Fall 1996).

School of Music and Art, Baltimore's Poly-Technical High School and the Illinois Mathematics and Science Academy, have transformed ordinary students into extraordinary ones by bolstering academic achievement through individual talents.

**Red Clay, DE**, and **Charlotte-Mecklenburg, NC**, have found magnet schools to be a powerful tool to create and then maintain racial integration without forced busing. Magnets attract students (and teachers) for what they do, not where they are, and have the demonstrated capacity to attract youngsters of all backgrounds and races.

Red Clay, in anticipation of being released from its court order, began to experiment with magnet programs at the middle school level, creating the Phoenix Academy, the Cab Calloway School of the Arts, and the Banking and Finance Academy. Focus groups and meetings with parents had convinced Red Clay consultants that the community was eager to end forced busing but at the same time was eager to keep the gains of racial integration. Magnets were the preferred tool. Red Clay — along with all of Wilmington — was released from the court order and returned to unitary status in 1996. Two of the middle school magnet programs will end when the classes graduate, and two elementary magnets (at Lewis and Shortlidge) were to open in September 1997. The Cab Calloway magnet program will be expanded to include high school and will be housed in the same building (the old

## IN GUILFORD

## REORGANIZING FOR CHANGE

In **Guilford, ME**, meeting lofty academic standards means making radical changes in the mundane affairs of daily life. It means thinking about how everyone from the superintendent and board members to teachers and students spends his or her time — and then throwing out these old roles and schedules and starting fresh.

In 1989, Guilford's board hired a superintendent, Raymond Poulin, who was eager to "set people free." Poulin organized the district with a corporate decision-making strategy, with himself as CEO and school board members as policy setters, not micromanagers. He supported site-based management by encouraging principals to see them-

selves as division managers and teachers to see themselves as client representatives. The business model demanded risk-taking to meet goals. "Everyone had to identify goals," says Norm Higgins, who succeeded Poulin when Poulin moved on to become Maine's assistant commissioner of education.

Wilmington High) with Delaware's first charter school, an open enrollment mathematics–science academy. **Red Clay, DE**, also opened Delaware's first public Montessori school in September 1997.

Let teachers choose as well. Teachers have different backgrounds and strengths, different ways of working, and different skills and interests, too. Most districts, however, tell teachers where and how to teach regardless of their personal preferences. Choice allows teachers to assume their rightful role as professional educators. Imagine the commitment when a teacher is able to pick and be picked by a school. Choice is a literal spark that ignites the creative minds of educators.

## USE TIME DIFFERENTLY

At first glance, the school day seems full. Look a little closer and ways to gain time for academics become obvious. Cut out annoying loudspeaker announcements and other interruptions. Cut out time spent changing classes and in assemblies, pep rallies, study halls and driver education. And rededicate the time to the core subjects of literature, mathematics, science, history, geography, second languages and the arts.

The tiresome 55-minute (or even less in some systems) course period in secondary schools needs attention, too. Students and teachers just get rolling when the bell rings. In rapid succession, for six or seven periods, students advance from mathematics to English to science to history to physical education, one class unconnected to the other. In the real world, disciplines are richly connected. Students and teachers are hungry for learning climates that are more natural, where lessons are mutually supportive with time for reflection, inquiry and debate. Compressing courses into half- or full-day sessions taught for shorter periods of the year is one idea.

Modular, college-type scheduling is another. Consider allowing classes to meet for extended periods two to three times a week as opposed to shorter periods for five days a week. Blocking certain subjects such as English and mathematics for extended periods in the morning is another option. Block scheduling paves the way for team teaching, working with students alternately in large or small groups, and regrouping students across grades and

COMPRESSING COURSES INTO HALF- OR FULL-DAY SESSIONS TAUGHT FOR SHORTER PERIODS OF THE YEAR IS ONE IDEA.

classes. Greater flexibility in the schedule will make it easier for schools to take advantage of the many instructional resources in their backyard — libraries, workplaces and youth group services.

### Extend Learning (Not Just School) Time

Already, traditional subjects seem to be squeezed into the school day. But if students are to meet new, ambitious standards and master new core curriculum, they'll need additional hours and days of learning time. Issues and concepts formerly reserved for the few must now be taught to the many. That means school districts must find the resources to keep schools open for business day in and day out, year-round. The best source on this issue is the 1994 report, _Prisoners of Time_, and its case studies by the National Education

## IN MURFREESBORO

## CASON LANE ACADEMY — A DREAM COME TRUE

Cason Lane Academy is the latest remarkable development in the remarkable school district of **Murfreesboro, TN.** Directed by Susan Genrich-Cameron, former Tennessee Teacher of the Year, Cason Lane Academy enrolls 950 children in an extended-day, extended-year school. The school officially opens at 6 a.m. and closes at 7 p.m. five days a week. Often it is open until 10 p.m. and on weekends, and it has just five holidays: Christmas, New Year's Day, Easter, Independence Day and Labor Day (unless parents petition to keep the building open). The open-enrollment school, by public demand a K–8 school in a K–6 district, draws students from around the district. And it is both site managed and site budgeted;

dollars flow from central office to Cason Lane on a per-pupil basis. Other income it "earns" (for example, from after-school programs). The school spends money and time as it sees fit. In short, Cason Lane has all the freedom and flexibility of a private school with the obligations and commitments of a public school.

How does Cason Lane invest its time and money? When teachers discovered that the site-management and site-budgeting rhetoric was real, they first insisted that the academic day be "protected." By this they meant no interruptions. No public address system announcements. No assemblies. No breaks. Pure academic time, every day from 8 a.m. to lunch. Day in and day out. Next, they opened their doors to

seventh- and eighth-graders, in response to overwhelming community disappointment with middle school.

The third step the director and teachers took was, in many respects, the most dramatic. To acquire more than $100,000 in funding for a technology program to improve reading and mathematics instruction, the school decided to forgo filling teaching vacancies, accumulating the savings until enough funds were available. Because Cason Lane Academy is in charge of its own professional life, time and money, Genrich-Cameron proudly reported the strategy to the full school board (and to the community, since meetings are televised) to keep it informed, not to obtain its approval.

Commission on Time and Learning. These reports, among other things, describe how to "reclaim the academic day."

Even without a large outlay of funds, some schools — such as those in **Murfreesboro, TN** — are moving to year-round schedules. In place of long summer vacations, year-round schedules provide shorter holidays more evenly spaced throughout the year. As a result, learning becomes a seamless process buoyed by the momentum of continuous instruction. The shorter the breaks, the more children remember what they learned before.

### The Right Questions: Reorganizing for Change

Facing up to high standards for all is a first step; communities must ask every question anew and sweep aside preconceptions about how they organize schools, manage instruction and use time. As you decide how to reorganize, consider these questions:

- What's fair about creating one kind of school and one kind of teaching style when children's interests and learning styles differ so vividly?

- If we are determined to vary the pedagogy and not the substance, don't we have to give children, parents and teachers choice among schools?

- Does it make sense to give the fastest and slowest students in a particular subject area identical time to master the same material?

- Why do the school day and year need to be the same length for everyone?

- Must we continue to measure courses in hours studied?

- Why not measure students by what they learn and give them the hours and days they need to master the material?

- How can we cling to the idea that education begins and ends at the school-house door? In fact, the public stake in children begins before birth and continues after the school day, through vacations and into adulthood.

## RETHINK TEACHER DEVELOPMENT

When we reorganize schools to emphasize standards and assessments, we must allow adequate time and training for teachers to implement the changes. How can a teacher be expected to do a good job when there is no time outside of class to prepare and correct lessons, hone skills, consult with other teachers or attend to all the matters that arise in a typical day?

Teachers are not born, they are made. None of us would fly with a pilot who had not spent years at the elbow of skilled aviators or accept treatment from a doctor who had not worked under the close supervision of experienced physicians. Yet we are willing to submit our children to teachers who have spent only a short time practice-teaching with little or no follow-up. Contrast that to first-year Japanese teachers who get an annual minimum of 20 days of in-service training — by law (**Stevenson and Stigler**). Contrast that to pilots and doctors who, after extensive apprenticeships, must continue to hone their skills and keep up with new developments or technologies in their field. Teachers cannot teach what they do not know.

Teaching is one of the learned professions, yet the working conditions in too many instances feel more blue-collar than white-collar. Confined to the four walls of one classroom every day; isolated from each other; no private office, no telephone access; no time to confer with colleagues; no freedom to shape curricula or choose instructional materials; charged with bus, corridor, cafeteria and playground duty on top of teaching loads — it's little wonder that the teaching force in America turns over rapidly.

Course content cannot be strengthened by fiat. Schools must equip teachers with new skills or else mandates for higher levels of achievement are doomed. To hand teachers standards booklets and expect them to digest and incorporate standards into their daily teaching regimen is unrealistic and counterproductive. Many believe that the only sound use of teachers' time is in front of the class, that researching, planning and collaborating with other professionals are a waste. In fact, the opposite is true: Lack of in-service training is a barrier to real reform. According to a study by the RAND corporation, new teaching strategies can require as much as 50 hours of instruction, practice and coaching before teachers master them. But according to a 1997 study by the **National Commission on Teaching and America's Future**, U.S. school districts spend less than 1 percent of their resources on staff development, compared with 8 percent to 10 percent in most corporations and foreign schools. Elementary school teachers have only 8.3 minutes of preparation time for every hour of teaching, and high school teachers have 13 minutes per hour of teaching time.

# TEACHERS AND THEIR UNIONS

Are teacher unions a plus or a minus when it comes to standards-based reform? As George Will says, the question reflects the "fallacy of the false alternative." No such dichotomy, no such either/or exists. The real question is how can school boards, administrators and teachers create a win–win situation? The short answer is that teachers must be a central part of the reform, or there will be no reform. The discussion must move beyond whether or not teachers are an asset or liability; the thoughtful manager knows that they are assets, plain and simple. As management expert Peter Drucker observes, there is no such thing as a bad worker, only a worker out of place.

There are, of course, other dimensions to the story. Bob Chase, the new head of the **National Education Association** (NEA), addressing the National Press Club, called for a "reinvention" of the union. Referring to his resistance to former President Mary Hatwood Futrell's attempt to mobilize the union to lead the reform movement, he said, "That was the biggest mistake of my career. And today, with all due respect, I say to the traditionalists in NEA's ranks, to those who argue that we should stick to our knitting, leaving education reform to others: You are mistaken."

The old industrial union model does not reflect the needs of the modern school. If school is not a factory, the important issues of compensation, seniority and due process must be rethought. Also important are new professional roles — teachers must be key actors in developing and implementing standards and assessments just as they must play a key role in curriculum development, textbook selection and other ways to guarantee ownership and ensure quality. Examples of such effective union–management collaboration have come about in Toledo, OH; Rochester, NY; Cincinnati, OH; Dade County, FL; Seattle, WA; Hammond, IN; and many other districts throughout the country. School boards set policy, but they need the benefit of teachers' expertise as they move forward.

Under a standards-driven system, teachers — and the unions that represent them — gain control of their professional lives. In exchange, they can expect to be accountable for professional behavior. Setting standards and creating relevant assessments are major steps forward in this process, and no one was a more eloquent spokesman for this than Al Shanker, the late **American Federation of Teachers** (AFT) president. If more evidence is needed, the lessons from the private for-profit sector are abundant and clear: To increase productivity and output (and to improve morale), push decision-making to the worker and hold workers accountable for results. No one knows more about the

*continued on page 94*

*continued from page 93*

## TEACHERS AND THEIR UNIONS

nature of work – and how to improve it – than the worker.

As long as schools are organized by districts, overseen by a board of trustees and run by professional administrators, legitimate and serious areas of disagreements are inevitable. But by tackling disagreements head on and negotiating in good faith and with mutual respect, progress is not just possible, it is probable. Something happens when people sit eye to eye and have a chance to lay their concerns on the table. Not unlike when engaging the publics of education (outlined in Step 1), areas of agreement surface. While participants may not change their own positions on an issue, their opinions of others' opinions often change – spawning new insights, new ways of seeing problems and new ways of acting together. And according to Adam Urbanski, president of the Rochester, NY, Teachers Association and a vice president of the AFT, "When we increase the chances for all students to learn better, everyone gains. It is both our moral imperative and in our enlightened self-interest."

If they hope to have their students achieving at much higher levels, school districts will have to deal with these sobering realities.

### Provide On-the-Job Training

More of the same isn't the answer. We should advance teacher training beyond the wearisome workshop where staffs come *en masse* to a one-shot session without regard to their individual levels of professional development or specific areas of need. Instead, we need to offer professional training that is highly focused and incorporated into the regular school day. Staff development ought to be indistinguishable from what teachers "do." Actual work activities — learning by doing the real thing — tied to finding the best ways to implement the standards are far superior to any canned workshop.

Teachers will tell you that the most important insights come from interactions with other teachers. Teachers need time to be in and out of one another's rooms, critiquing lessons and picking up pointers. They need time to work with other teachers and time to plan and polish instructional lessons. (In Japan, teachers may take a whole year to refine one lesson.) They need time to gather the accumulated wisdom of generations of skilled practitioners. They need time to read professional journals, get on the Internet and watch outstanding teachers demonstrate new strategies. Most of all, teachers need time to tap into their versatility, energy and inventiveness — time to reflect on the practice of teaching.

An in-school approach will allow teachers to take advantage of daily opportunities for professional development, tailored to their needs, with immediate and sustained reinforcement and feedback. To make this happen, districts need to devote time and resources to planning and professional development — not as a frill or an add-on, but as a central component to the agreement between teachers and districts.

## How the Central Office Can Help

Form follows function, structure serves policy. At least they should. As a district transits into a performance-driven mode, its administrative and organizational arrangements should change. An effective system of standards and assessments means that schools must be free to pursue their goals according to their own lights — and be held accountable for meeting their standards. In such a district, headquarters becomes a service center, not a command center; it provides whatever schools need to meet their objectives. In its most advanced form, headquarters would actually "sell" its services to schools and be forced to meet a market test. Some charter schools already do this; they receive a full per-pupil allotment and buy the administrative and special services they do not provide themselves.

To accomplish this transformation in teacher training, the central office needs to change its role here as well. Rather than doling out staff development as it sees fit, the central office needs to provide the services, resources and technology that schools demand. Academic standards should be the driving force for teacher training. **Red Clay, DE**, for example, is providing elementary school teachers with training for a science curriculum tied to new higher standards. Teachers recognize the relevance of the training to what they do every day in their classrooms — and they're clamoring for more training. In **Murfreesboro, TN**, the district is using the results of state and local academic achievement tests to target staff development more effectively and to challenge principals to develop plans to improve results.

Districts can help in several ways: Give the most accomplished teachers higher pay, reduced teaching loads and more time to mentor colleagues; extend the contract year to pay teachers for professional development; use the longer day for the same purpose; or use a cadre of well-prepared, full-time, substitute teachers to fill in for teachers as they observe model lessons. Relieving teachers of lunch, playground and bus duty by supplying schools with a troupe of less costly aides is another promising alternative. Or try a radical approach: Build a bank of time for teachers by requiring everyone in central administration to teach or assist in a school to help lighten teacher loads.

## IN BEAUFORT

# HIGH TECHNOLOGY AT SCHOOL AND AT HOME

A quick and semi-scientific survey on Hilton Head Island (home to four **Beaufort County, SC**, schools and the wealthiest part of the county; indeed, one of the wealthiest enclaves in South Carolina) revealed that four-fifths of the children had access to computers at home while only one-fifth of the teachers did. There was no lack of desire to own computers among faculty and other school staff members, but there were questions of money and knowledge, such as what kind of computer to buy and what it would cost.

The answers came from the district, which extended its purchasing power to the board and staff. Anyone who works for the system is able to buy the "Beaufort package" at cost, using payroll deductions over time if they prefer.

The scheme does more than make computers affordable, however – anyone who buys one gets what the schools get: a fast computer loaded with common software and a modem. There is no compatibility problem; everyone can swap disks, use central printers and scanners, e-mail each other and access the Internet. In one fell swoop, the district has begun a do-it-yourself district-wide network, a virtual school district that parallels the real one.

Decisions about computer use in the schools are not much different. With the passage of a $122-million bond issue, computers will be available to every student and every teacher in every building in the district, but they will not be distributed helter-skelter like textbooks and chalk. No school gets a single computer until it has completed a technology plan that lays out how new technologies will improve learning and increase academic accomplishment. The technology plan must be approved by the superintendent, and the principal and staff then present it to the school board for approval. It's a learning process for everyone, from kids to board members. To date, six schools have had their plans approved, and their staffs are being trained as the computers are installed (along with fiber optic networks). Six additional schools have received initial approval and fiber optic cable was to be in place by late spring 1997. The remaining six plans were expected to be approved by fall 1997.

## WHO WILL PAY FOR TRAINING?

Financially strapped districts will have problems paying for training, as they do for everything. Fortunately, most districts have the resources to provide a number of days of in-service training and in the heat of change can squeeze out additional resources. They may turn to the state, return to their own budgets, look for financial support from outside foundations — all the usual routes.

But every district can afford to pay the teachers to develop new standards and assessments. Indeed, this process is the single most powerful staff development tool we have ever encountered. It is a wise and relatively inexpensive investment.

As schools look for funds, however, they should keep in mind one truth: No successful modern corporation could run effectively on the Spartan diet of training that most school districts live on. Every employee at Xerox, IBM, Corning, Kodak and a growing number of companies receives at least two weeks of training a year. The reason is not to make employees feel good (though it often does) or to offer an opportunity to have fun (though training often is); corporations train because training pays for itself in increased productivity. Training will do the same thing in schools — and school districts should turn to business partners to help make that case.

Districts also can use resources wisely and creatively as **Beaufort County, SC**, has done in making computers available to teachers and staffs.

The central office can offer a school architecture that supports collegiality and professionalism. German and Japanese schools, for instance, are equipped with teachers' rooms large enough to provide each teacher with a desk. Teachers spend their off hours here perfecting lessons, correcting papers and discussing teaching strategies with peers. Staffs meet often, as a whole, to improve lesson plans and share new and better instructional techniques. It's an everyday occurrence for teachers to observe their colleagues in action (**Stevenson and Stigler**). We need to provide our teachers the same opportunities — American style.

In addition, districts can encourage their teachers to apply for certification by the **National Board for Professional Teaching Standards**, which establishes

## NURTURING A CULTURE FOR CHANGE

School culture should support cooperation, improvement and new ways of doing things. In **Beaufort County, SC**, Superintendent Herman Gaither sets the tone: "You are not allowed to step on other people to get ahead; you must go around them." By this he means that he won't tolerate principals or teachers complaining about colleagues to make themselves look better — or to make excuses for their own performance.

In **Guilford, ME**, Superintendent Norm Higgins believes in giving people time to accept change. "I take great exception to people who say, 'If people don't get on board, the train is leaving without them.' I say, 'This is like a model railroad. The train keeps going around, and you can get on board anytime. We'll reward those who are with us, but we won't punish those who are not with us.'"

high standards for what teachers should know and be able to do, and is developing a system of advanced, voluntary assessments.

School districts also may want to consider a teachers' academy, staffed by expert practitioners, to replace the prevailing system. There, teachers would take turns mastering the latest instructional techniques and materials and return to their home schools to pass the good word on to their colleagues. Learning would become continuous. In a professional setting, teachers would learn how to tailor instruction to students' needs; how to group students flexibly, creatively and effectively; how to overhaul reading, writing and mathematics programs in short order; and how to monitor student progress via test data.

## GIVE PRINCIPALS NEW LEADERSHIP AND MANAGEMENT SKILLS

Reaching and sustaining high academic achievement are not the responsibility of teachers alone. Principals, too, need to understand and support new ways of working. In **Red Clay, DE**, elementary school teachers are implementing a challenging new science curriculum for which they've received extensive training in state-of-the-art, thematic units from the Smithsonian. But when a principal walks into a classroom where students are learning about earth science and sees what he perceives as kids playing with dirt — and tells the teacher he'll come back when she's *really* teaching them something — the message to teachers is discouraging, to say the least.

Outstanding schools need outstanding principals — but the definition of an outstanding principal is changing as students, teachers and schools change. The emergence of site-based management, shared decision-making, increasingly diverse school populations and an intense focus on education results require those who lead schools to demonstrate a new set of skills. Schools call for a wide range of instructional, supervisory and administrative competencies. Principals — both new and mature — need training and the opportunity to grab hold of the latest instructional and management techniques to stay current and support higher academic goals.

Principals should have a grasp of the content and skills to be taught in various subject areas to be true instructional leaders. Once a principal knows what good instruction looks like and has a solid plan for school improvement, the critical element is assessing and monitoring the school program. Thus, principals need to be able to analyze data and monitor the implementation of selected improvement strategies. Poor communication with the staff and the broader community is another downfall of many principals. Beyond learning how to create solid relationships, win–win resolutions to sticky problems and ways of involving parents are worth a training session or two.

Traditional university programs tend to provide a sound base of knowledge about school administration, but they fall short in linking theory and research with practice. Even the best courses do not supply the level of skill and the practical understanding that come from working directly with school staffs and students in the classroom. Top-line professional training — whatever the vocation — has two basic elements: deep grounding in the content of the discipline and hands-on experience under the direct guidance of a seasoned practitioner.

To ensure depth and perspective, courses dealing with professional practice should be co-taught by university professors and veteran school administrators. Be sure to enlist successful principals who can divulge their unique approaches to organizing schools for academic success. As successful school management is driven by the lessons of the marketplace and best practices —

standards, outputs, benchmarks, accountability, innovation and competition — running a school is similar to running a business. That means asking business experts to join ranks with educators to train principals. Class sessions could alternate between meetings at the university and school visitations to classrooms of exemplary teachers. Between visitations, participants could be assigned homework to put what they've learned into practice.

> ➤ **Six essential skills for principals (from Charlotte-Mecklenburg, NC, schools)**

## Set Up a System for Continuous Learning

Principals in **Charlotte-Mecklenburg, NC**, under Murphy's leadership, were continually refreshing and expanding their knowledge and skills. Ongoing leadership training gave principals a chance to hear firsthand from the movers and shakers in education — the national experts who were blazing the trail. Taking a day every month or every other month to meet with their peers and debate the issues one-on-one with the experts improved performance and lifted spirits. Through such seminars, principals picked up tips from national experts that they in turn brought back to their staffs.

Charlotte-Mecklenburg principals, especially those failing to make the grade, got opportunities to fine-tune the fundamentals in a range of seminars, study groups, conferences and individual tutorials. Throughout the year, Charlotte-Mecklenburg offered intensives for principals weak in more than one area. Several more successful principals ran the sessions and shared how they were getting the job done. University and business personnel assisted with the workshops.

Small skills groups give principals ample opportunity for immediate reinforcement and feedback, as well as the opportunity to bond with colleagues. Principals are assigned to the training that best serves their needs as determined by annual evaluation data. They come away from professional development with concrete solutions and promising strategies. Common themes emerge. Some principals have trouble with shared decision-making, others are weak in data analysis. Some want help with discipline issues, teacher evaluations or parental communications. Under this system, training is tailored to the principal.

> ➤ **Principals' training program**

# MEASURING UP

## Holding Students Accountable

What gets measured gets taught. What gets tested gets emphasized. Properly used, tests have a remarkably positive effect on learning. A good test keeps everyone — grown-ups and youngsters alike — focused on the right stuff. Good measures keep instruction on track. In the classroom, they give the teacher critical feedback to determine whether students have mastered their lessons and are ready for new ones. They are useful in designing and prescribing new and better interventions. They make it possible to measure the performance of teachers, schools and students. For the student, tests create an opportunity for additional learning. And most important, because they certify performance for advancement or graduation, they capture students' attention. Students always ask, "Does this count?"

Without good tests, young people can't know if they've learned what they need to learn; parents can't keep track of their child's progress; teachers can't adjust instruction appropriately; districts can't judge the effectiveness of their programs. Imagine purchasing a house without an inspection report, managing a business without monthly profit and loss statements, undergoing surgery without trustworthy health information or launching a weight-loss campaign without carefully calibrated scales and tape measure in hand. We simply wouldn't do it.

## DEVELOP BETTER TESTS

Once school districts develop content and performance standards, taking stock of existing tests and, as necessary, supplementing current assessments with new ones are the next priority. In the process, districts need to look at several key issues to make informed choices:

* How will each test be used? For diagnostic purposes, to help teachers modify instruction to help each student reach the standards? Or for accountability purposes, to hold the student, the teacher, the school or the district accountable for performance?

**AT A GLANCE**

* Develop better tests
* Use a mix of tests
* Involve teachers
* Give people time to adjust

## PERFORMANCE STANDARDS

Performance standards are not new to education. The nation's — perhaps the world's — best language school, the Foreign Service Institute, has used them for decades in its programs. Using an internationally recognized scale (0 to 5+), students and teachers are ranked on what they know and can do. A simultaneous translator needs to be ranked 5+; a commercial attaché may do his or her job as a 3+; a tourist can get around with a 1+ or get around better as a 2+. The Foreign Service Institute gives no grades, just defined ratings; time is the flexible variable. A student studies until he or she achieves a level of mastery consistent with the prospective assignment.

The time it takes to become fluent is interesting from the standpoint of resource allocation; someone who has a lower aptitude or poor motivation may take twice as long as a colleague to reach the same level of proficiency. But the fact remains: Measured and certified mastery is a better metric than a grade or seat time.

- What mix of tests do you want to accomplish your purposes? Norm-referenced tests show how students in a given class, school, group or school system are doing compared with other students. Criterion- or standards-referenced tests, on the other hand, measure the extent to which students master specific skills and knowledge.

- Do you want to use multiple-choice tests or more open-ended, performance-based tests?

- Do you want to use your own tests? The state's tests? Tests developed by others such as the College Board or **New Standards**™?

For more on standards, see Step 2.

For more on accountability, see Step 6.

### Norm-Referenced Tests vs. Standards-Referenced Tests

*Norm-referenced tests,* such as the California Test of Basic Skills or the Stanford Achievement Test, are familiar to most of us. New assessments that can tell us how well students are performing against specific standards are called *standards-referenced exams.* Their precursors were called criterion-referenced tests, tests tied directly to the curriculum. While many people use these terms interchangeably, standards-referenced exams, by definition, almost always include a mixture of multiple-choice, short-answer and performance-based tasks. Criterion-referenced tests tend to include only the first two.

Norm-referenced tests are very limited in assessing how much students have learned and the extent to which student work meets the standard or falls short. Instead, norm-referenced tests compare students to students. Norm-referenced tests have some advantages. If they are administered year after year, they show how students of different races, genders and socio-economic groups are faring over time. They help measure the effectiveness of specific district, school and instructional programs. And they reveal where the curriculum is strong and weak.

But norm-referenced tests don't tell us whether students are meeting the standards. Scores are reported in terms of percentile ranks, which reveal only how a student is ranked in relation to the performance of other students who took the test. (A 60th percentile rating does not mean that the student answered 60 percent of the questions correctly.) Just what does "average performance" or "above average performance" mean? Regardless of others' performance, what does Jack actually know about mathematics? What does Jane actually know about science? What can he or she do with this knowledge? Norm-referenced tests don't answer those questions.

Standard-referenced exams, on the other hand, provide detailed information about the specific skills and knowledge that individual students master. Common examples are the **Advanced Placement** exams of the College Board and the **International Baccalaureate** exams. Tests such as these tell teachers, students and parents, item by item, what a student knows and can do — and what a student has yet to learn. At the classroom level, standards-referenced tests help teachers make informed decisions about grouping students, reducing or extending time allocated to a unit, changing instructional strategies and modifying instructional materials.

## Multiple-Choice or Performance-Based Tests?

Everyone is familiar with multiple-choice tests, where students select the right answer from a menu of possible answers. Their advantages are obvious. They're easy and inexpensive to administer and score, and they're very reliable. Moreover, and contrary to conventional wisdom, good multiple-choice tests can challenge students to solve complex problems and demonstrate their mastery of the subject. Indeed, the most respected test in the United States — the **National Assessment of Educational Progress** — relies heavily on multiple-choice problems.

However, many states and districts now are supplementing their multiple-choice tests with performance-based assessments, which are aligned with their new content standards. Written essays are the most common example, but increasingly these include actual demonstrations (like science experiments); performances (like a one-act play); the completion of complex, long-term assignments (like designing a working robot); or portfolios of student work, which include a wide range of materials from tests to lengthy reports, usually compiled over an entire school year. The states of **Maryland**, Vermont, **Delaware** and Kentucky, as well as **New Standards**™, have been especially active in piloting these alternative assessments.

Their benefits are clear. On multiple-choice tests, students can get the right answer by merely guessing correctly; performance-based exams typically require students to describe the thinking that went into the answer. They also allow students to showcase new ideas or hypotheses. Longer, more complex tasks require students to actually demonstrate what they know and can do, to apply their knowledge to solve problems — for example, to write a persuasive letter to the editor instead of just knowing the rules of grammar.

But performance-based tests have drawbacks as well. The College Board began using multiple-choice tests because performance-based tests were not as accurate. Performance-based tests tend to depend more on which year a student takes the exam or on who grades the test than on the skill or competency demonstrated. Despite substantial training, tests are often scored differently by different people on different occasions; unreliability is inherent. In addition, these tests tend to cover less content and are much more expensive to develop and to grade. Teachers need extensive professional development before they are qualified to administer and score performance-based tests.

## For Diagnostic or Accountability Purposes?

As you develop a new set of exams, determine the purpose. For each test, ask if you will use it for diagnosis or accountability. If the answer is for accountability, is the test to measure school performance or individual achievement? The answers will have an impact on how each test is designed and used and how results are reported. **Charlotte-Mecklenburg, NC**, and **Beaufort County, SC**, for instance, are using their new standards-referenced tests for diagnosis only. At the school level, staffs look at what concepts and skills each student has attained and what needs to be done to get the student's work to the standard.

These districts then use external measures to hold individual students and schools accountable. State end-of-course tests hold students accountable, and norm-referenced tests hold schools accountable. Tests such as these, which carry high consequences for students and staffs, have been shown to spur effort. But teachers also need tests that give comprehensive information about a student's progress in attaining the standard so instruction can be tailored accordingly.

The best bet is to use several levels and types of referenced testing, all geared to measure student mastery of the standards. Districts must take care not to overtest students, but asking a single test to satisfy all purposes is a mistake. One source of information provides only a snapshot of student strengths and needs; multiple indicators provide an enhanced picture and a better chance of meeting students' needs.

### For School or Student Accountability?

Again, there are tradeoffs. When school improvement is the focus, no one child has to take all parts of each test, reducing the amount of testing time. You can test some students on some items within a content area and other students on other items and still have a statistically significant result that can be used to alter the curriculum and instruction.

The downside to school accountability tests is that some students will continue to be passed on grade to grade until they find out the hard way — through low grades, college rejections or low-paying jobs — that failing to learn has consequences.

On the other hand, student accountability tests have high stakes. Students know that these tests count; schools use them to place students in special instructional programs, to decide whether students are ready to advance to the next grade or, ultimately, to graduate. These tests make it much less likely that any student will slide by. One relative disadvantage of using tests to hold individuals accountable is that students have to be tested on all items instead of a sample, which means additional testing time.

DISTRICTS MUST TAKE CARE NOT TO OVERTEST STUDENTS, BUT ASKING A SINGLE TEST TO SATISFY ALL PURPOSES IS A MISTAKE.

## SPOTLIGHT

# SEND A SIGNAL TO STUDENTS

Clear and rigorous standards will be welcome news to businesses and colleges alike, but unless standards connect directly to graduation requirements, not much will have been accomplished. Only in New York state, which awards a Regents Diploma, does confidence in the high school diploma remain high. As it turns out, that confidence is well placed. New York has among the highest Scholastic Assessment Test scores in the nation, a direct consequence of demanding curriculum and demanding measures — at least for a portion of its students.

Districts and teachers encounter intense pressure not to fail or "hold back" students, whether they have mastered the material or not. Though the diploma remains a necessary credential for employment and school admission, few employers pore over transcripts to determine evidence of authentic academic achievement. Even those determined few aren't likely to be enlightened. Course titles reveal little about true content. Course grades don't tell much more; high grades in easy courses mean less than low grades in rigorous ones. Moreover, teachers grade differently. Some pass students onto the next grade without requiring students to learn very much; others require a lot.

These points aren't lost on students. They know they can graduate without working very hard or learning very much. Simply putting higher standards in front of students, without giving them palpable reasons to strive for them, is an exercise in futility. The quickest way to improve schools is to make what students do in them count, namely design a diploma that means something — one that reflects real mastery — and tie student promotion to rigorous assessments.

➢ **Information about what the Business Coalition for Education Reform is doing to send a signal to students that school counts**

Overall, we favor tests that focus on individual accountability. In the real world, individuals face the consequences of their actions and reap the rewards for their achievements. Businesses hire individuals; colleges select individuals. If individuals improve, schools will improve. If we hold individuals accountable, we can hold schools accountable. The opposite is not true. Passing a single, external, on-demand assessment in a content area should not be the sole measure of competency. One idea worth considering, used by our counterparts across the sea, is to give double weight to exam scores, then average them with course grades to yield an overall score.

# HOW OTHER COUNTRIES TEST

| Country | Exam Length | Question Type | Breadth vs. Depth | Scope of the Examination System | Additional Graduation Requirements |
|---------|-------------|---------------|-------------------|----------------------------------|-----------------------------------|
| France | Two and a half hours per subject. | Open-ended questions from a few words to multiple-paragraph essays. | Exams require students to go into considerable detail on a small number of topics, but curriculum is broad. | Take written exams in three required subjects (mathematics, French and history/geography). | Exam scores are double weighted and then averaged with course grades to yield an overall score. Must satisfactorily complete coursework in 11 subjects. |
| Germany | Two to four hours per subject. | Open-ended questions from a few words to multiple-paragraph essays. | Exams require students to go into considerable detail on a small number of topics, but curriculum is broad. | Take written exams in three required subjects (mathematics, German and English). Must complete oral exams in two additional subjects. | Must earn passing grades in all courses in the last two years of school and pass the exams. Exam scores are listed on the graduation certificate. |
| Scotland | One to two and a half hours per subject. | Open-ended questions from a few words to multiple-paragraph essays. | Exams require students to go into considerable detail on a small number of topics, but curriculum is broad. | Students choose the number of exams to take and in what subjects, but most take four (English, mathematics, a science and a foreign language). Exams come in three levels: credit (most advanced), general and foundation (least advanced). | Must pass one exam to receive a certificate. Exam scores are listed on the graduation certificate as added incentive. |

Source: <u>American Federation of Teachers</u>, *Standards Review*, 1996

*The table above illustrates how other countries blend exam scores with course grades in different ways to yield a richer portrait of student achievement.*

## Can a New Assessment Serve Two Masters?

While schools can use the new assessments both to improve instruction and to hold staffs accountable, teachers may find using the tests mainly for instructional purposes difficult if the tests also are being used to evaluate schools and staffs. Peculiarities in test administration and overzealous coaching can result. Instituting two kinds of assessments is best for schools: one assessment used strictly for instruction and student accountability and the other for staff accountability.

## USE A MIX OF TESTS

What's a district to do? First, rather than abolish objective tests, insist on more demanding ones. The bar examination for lawyers and the **Advanced Placement** test — two of the most exacting assessments used today — have hefty multiple-choice components (50 percent), proof that rigor and objective tests are not irreconcilable. The **National Assessment of Educational Progress**, a tough test designed to gauge higher-order skills, until recently consisted solely of multiple-choice items.

As these exams confirm, multiple-choice questions don't have to be dull or encourage rote learning. As **E.D. Hirsch** reminds us in his recent book, *The Schools We Need and Why We Don't Have Them*, the improper use of multiple-choice tests shouldn't preclude their proper use. Well-constructed and -designed objective tests of mathematics or reading exist. They require students to analyze and synthesize information, generate ideas, think critically, structure tasks and solve problems. The other test abuses, such as teacher coaching on specific questions, can be avoided easily by watchful educators, tight security and the creation of new questions or multiple forms of a test each year.

Second, rather than a single type of measure, build an integrated assessment that includes multiple-choice and short-answer questions as well as essays. This blend ensures accuracy and fairness at a reasonable cost. Mathematics tests can include a performance-based component by requiring students to display their computations on test papers. Alternately, writing tests can include a multiple-choice component.

# BENCHMARK AGAINST THE WORLD'S BEST

Standards and the tests used to measure them must permit comparisons – among schools in a district, among districts in a state and among schools in different states. Governors (and mayors) must be able to boast (or complain) about their academic standings as readily as they do football scores. Without the capacity to compare results with some precision, the standards-setting exercise will be an exercise in futility.

How can you be assured that your standards and assessments are rigorous and high? Use an external benchmark and compare yourself with gusto. Mark Musick, head of the Southern Regional Education Board and a member of the National Assessment Governing Board, uses three states to make the case:

- In State I, 59 percent of eighth graders passed the state mathematics test and met at least the minimum expectations. But only 21 percent reached the proficient or "good enough" level on the **National Assessment of Educational Progress** (NAEP), a highly regarded national test.

- In State II, where 62 percent of the eighth graders were "proficient" on the state test, only 15 percent were "proficient" when measured by the NAEP.

- In State III, 83 percent of eighth graders reached the state goal of "adequate and acceptable performance," and 40 percent reached the "excellence" level. But only 16 percent were "proficient" on the NAEP.

The results jolted these states, where educators thought they had replaced their minimum competency standards with new, high standards. Gaps between the two measures should sound the alarm and cause districts to reflect on the validity of measures. The NAEP "proficient" level is known for its rigor. If a high correlation exists between state or district tests and NAEP tests, you are on the right track. If 90 percent of students are passing district tests, while only 30 percent are able to achieve a satisfactory level in the same subject on the NAEP, then the district test – or the standards and implementation – is not rigorous enough.

You need not limit yourself to the NAEP. You can employ other external benchmarks such as those from **Maryland** and **Delaware**, states whose students score about the same on state tests as on the NAEP. Or, if you really want to think big, compare pass rates on international tests – to make certain your education standards and tests set high expectations.

# STEP 5

Finally, make sure to compare your tests to the best in the nation and the world. Low-level tests don't help students. At some point, students will compete against graduates from schools in other districts, states and nations — from communities that hold students to much higher standards of achievement. Guess who wins such competitions?

## Align Local and State Assessments

At a minimum, teachers should insist that local tests and standards comply with state mandates. Districts need to make sure their homegrown tests are at least as good as the state's — and that their students can pass state tests. Red Clay, DE, for example, is developing its new tests with a close eye on its own standards and the state's. State and local tests should complement one another. Each has strengths and weaknesses. State tests — which provide only a snapshot of performance — are unlikely to provide enough information to be used for diagnosis in the classroom.

## IN BEAUFORT

## STANDARDS-REFERENCED TESTS: CAN THEY BE HOMEGROWN?

The only people in the school building who hate tests as much as students are teachers; aside from an atavistic aversion to measurement, there are some sensible reasons teachers are leery about tests. If tests are imposed from on high, they may have little relationship to what teachers do in their classrooms; they may have no bearing on students' backgrounds and patterns of preparation; and they may employ norms that are badly out of date. Most important, tests are almost certain to be used to hold teachers and students up to

ridicule (or so it seems). Is there an answer to this set of fears?

A nearly complete answer is locally generated tests that are reliable and valid. They test what is taught (because they are aligned to the standards and curriculum); they reflect the teachers' and community's best thinking about what students should know and be able to do; they are diagnostic (thereby helping improve teaching and learning); and they are less likely to be used pejoratively.

Easy to say, hard to do — but Beaufort County, SC, is doing it. With the superintendent's active support and two years of hard work, district analyst Catherine McCaslin and her teams have produced readiness- and foundations-level English language arts tests and similar tests for mathematics. (Readiness and foundations levels are roughly equivalent to K–5, but as multi-age grouping becomes a reality, the old grade references become obsolete.) The test items were designed by teams of teachers who linked them,

*continued on page 111*

On the other hand, avoid an assessment system based solely on the judgments of individual classroom teachers. The problem here is that teachers seldom, if ever, have the opportunity to discuss common criteria for developing and scoring end-of-course tests. There is no common reference to judge students in different classes with different teachers in different schools. Sound comparisons across individuals, classrooms and schools are a must. That means developing district tests — with teacher input — tied directly to district standards and aligned with the state exam(s).

Teams of teachers are working on assessments in **Guilford, ME**, for example, but the district is bringing in outside experts to help them. Classroom teachers with computer aptitude are working with curriculum teams to pilot electronic assessments, which adds another dimension to this piece of work. "We're trying to learn from that particular group of teachers," Superintendent Norm Higgins says. "And we've been laying the electronic infrastructure in place so there won't be a delay in using the assessments when they're ready. It takes a bit of planning to think about when all these pieces are going to start."

*continued from page 110*

item by item, to the district's standards, producing, in those subjects for those grades, a true performance-based system of standards and measures.

After the test items and graphics were designed, they were sent to the district's test contractor (in Canada), who created the text and layout and integrated the audio and video into the standards-testing system (using a Beaufort voice-over). As the Beaufort teachers have become more familiar and expert with creating and then linking items to standards, they are ready to buy large item banks. The tests are all computer-based – multimedia, interactive – using voice or audio directions through individual earphones.

The new tests provide teachers with the freedom to test individual students on individual standards or groups of standards at will. They also can be used for continuous assessment and appropriate placement in reading and mathematics groups. The tests are self-contained and self-directed, allowing different tests to be used on different computers at different school sites at the same time. Their ready availability – whether schools have networks or stand-alone computer systems – makes continuous progress a reality.

Students at **Broad River Elementary School** and Port Royal (the only two schools fully up to speed) are in true performance-based groups for reading

and mathematics (no more heterogeneous grouping), and a child may move from advanced mathematics to less-advanced English (or the reverse) as he or she progresses. As exciting as the system is, it is not without its problems. Teachers accustomed to class groupings find "continuous progress" a bit daunting. Teachers used to testing kids in groups find the prospect (and practice) of testing individuals unfamiliar. McCaslin and her colleagues plan to take the 1997–98 year to consolidate before developing new tests for every subject and age group.

By all means, if you live in a state that still has low standards and low-level tests, don't wait for state officials to act. Develop your own standards and tests.

## INVOLVE TEACHERS

To develop fair methods of assessing students on topics that really matter, test developers should know what's important to subject-matter teachers and take enough time to work with them as equals. Whether you decide to build your own tests, buy item inventories or contract with outside testing firms for your local test, be sure the structure allows maximum teacher input. Without teacher input from beginning to end, there will be no credibility. One of the primary reasons people welcomed the new **Charlotte-Mecklenburg, NC**, and **Beaufort County, SC**, district tests into the school culture is that teachers helped to build them.

Full-scale involvement by teachers in every phase of development increases ownership and ensures ease of implementation. Investing in a cadre of teachers/developers who participate in and experiment with the proposed assessment at the student and school level is wise for several obvious reasons. Teacher involvement ensures that the tests are aligned with classroom curriculum. Just as on the content standards, teachers "own" the test. Moreover, the process of developing new tests is a powerful professional development tool.

### Benchmark Best Practices

No need to start from scratch. Districts should be thoroughly grounded in existing tests, with particular attention to states and school systems that have taken the lead in developing improved assessment systems for student credentialing. Study standards, exams and student work from a variety of states and districts to see what students are expected to learn, how well they are expected to learn it and how they are expected to demonstrate their knowledge. Kentucky, **Maryland** and **New Standards**™ are among the leaders in the field. One effective and inexpensive way to build up your stock of test items is to participate in test swap-meets with neighboring or like-minded jurisdictions.

➤ **Additional information and resources about assessments**

Charlotte-Mecklenburg teachers, for example, crafted new tests from test items purchased from several sources. They supplemented the test item lists with their own questions. As they checked the tests in the field, teachers worked alongside psychometricians to determine the validity and reliability of test questions and to revise the exams accordingly. Beaufort built its referenced exams from scratch and worried less about meeting psychometric principles.

If you're using tests developed by others, the key point is to make sure the test items are aligned to the district's specific standards and performance objectives, that teachers have the skills to administer and score them, and that what is taught in the classroom (the curriculum) is aligned to the tests.

## GIVE PEOPLE TIME TO ADJUST

Work with all deliberate speed, but rushing high-stakes exams into place too quickly can just as easily become a barrier to reform. Raising exit demands means

## READINESS, SMALL TIME

School readiness, particularly in a strikingly heterogeneous community like **Beaufort County, SC**, can be hard to assess. Yet as teachers and administrators know, accurately assessing readiness for incoming kindergartners and first graders is very important. Not only is it important to know who is ready for what, but children who are way behind are also eligible for special programs. Most commercial instruments are not satisfactory; moreover, in Beaufort, there is a strong inclination to solve problems locally.

Under the guidance of district analyst Catherine McCaslin, groups of teachers (with support from the central office) are assembling a Beaufort "Readiness for School" instrument by identifying those standards that are judged to be most important to school readiness and success. Designed to be used with a touch-screen computer, the readiness test solves the problem of measuring readiness with preliterate children. A voice-over supplied by a melodious teacher and bright colors were the first steps. Together with the new technology available in Beaufort, McCaslin and her colleagues developed a set of test questions in which they have confidence.

In many respects the process is as important as the product. For most of the Beaufort team, this was their first venture into test design and intensive computer use. In the first administration, the computers were awkward to set up — and a bit intimidating. (Not to the children; they loved them.) The format chosen by the team was inviting to students and useful to teachers, and it is continually being fine-tuned. Now into year three, not only does Beaufort have a better fix on student readiness, but it also has developed a powerful professional development tool.

that many students are likely to fail. Political pressure will be intense to "dumb down" exams so students used to passing will continue to pass and graduate.

To test before content standards are implemented, before performance standards are in place and before teachers are trained in their use is a mistake. Plan on working at least two to three years before you have tests on which high-stakes decisions can be made. The challenge is to put test implementation on as fast a track as is possible. Given a choice between having some sort of test in one year or a fair and rigorous test in three years, we favor the latter. On the other hand, make sure you set a clear timetable and push the envelope. New assessments raise fear, which can easily lead to foot-dragging.

<u>Maryland</u>, which has one of the most highly lauded testing programs in the nation, started its work in 1991. Five years into the process, Maryland is only now getting comfortable with the results. The <u>Maryland School Performance Assessment Program</u> is built around what students are supposed to be learning — standards for the year 2000. The fit between the test and student achievement has been improving. But all districts in Maryland except one are still performing at below-satisfactory levels, though marked improvement among individual schools is apparent.

You can prepare parents for the short-term pain (lower grades) in exchange for long-term gain (more capable students) with deliberate, careful and regular communication. Improvement will come more quickly to districts that hold the line as real consequences provoke action.

## Making Changes in the Classroom

Milwaukee, WI, is a case in point. *The Washington Post* (Feb. 26, 1997) examined the issue of academic standards and testing in Wisconsin and found that the state's efforts had sparked fierce debate and inspired self-reflection and an understanding that more work is required.

In 1995, Milwaukee developed a new mathematics test along with a policy that made passing the test a graduation requirement. The first results were dismal: 79 percent failed. People were really thrown by the results. According to the *Post*, these results did more than surprise parents and students; the results made them angry.

Rather than back down, the entire community rallied to help students do better. Instead of blaming the test, some school leaders pointed a finger at themselves. Teachers signaled their willingness to change their classroom habits. In response to calls from students, high schools started after-school and Saturday tutoring sessions in mathematics. The city shifted funds to help. Churches and businesses donated school supplies and identified volunteer tutors. Attendance at PTA meetings rose. Students changed their habits as well. As many students noted, they hadn't considered the new tests important because most tests have few, if any, consequences. Enlightened self-interest kicked in once they realized the state meant business. The effort paid off. After six months improvements were visible: 55 percent of the students passed the test the second time around.

Setting and meeting higher standards require schools districts to examine themselves critically. Diane Ravitch, a senior fellow at the Brookings Institution and former assistant secretary of education in the U.S. Department of Education, says, "Everyone wants high standards, but when schools get serious about it, they tend to get a cold splash in the face. What they risk finding is that an extraordinary number of kids do not measure up." To that, we add: Stand strong and lasting results will be yours. If Milwaukee can do it ...

## Academic Decathlon

Another solution to the political problem of likely failures is to differentiate the diploma system, as the New York State Regents does. Students who take these exams and score high enough earn a special advanced diploma that's recognized nationally. Making the exams optional has helped New York resist the pressure to "dumb down" expectations. On the other hand, keeping the exams optional hasn't motivated all students to work hard and achieve. In fact, New York is phasing in the Regents courses and exams as a graduation requirement for *all* students.

Another option exists, however. We call it the academic decathlon. For districts that set standards in a range of content areas — mathematics, language arts, science, history, geography, economics, foreign language, workplace skills and the arts — the academic decathlon means adopting a "matrix of mastery" diploma. Holding tight to rigorous standards in reading,

**RATHER THAN BACK DOWN FROM ACADEMIC STANDARDS, THE MILWAUKEE COMMUNITY RALLIED TO HELP STUDENTS DO BETTER.**

writing, mathematics and science while giving students some choice about what other subject areas to pursue in depth is an option.

With the academic decathlon's 10 subject areas and five developmental levels of learning in each (for example, basic, proficient, advanced and honors), students could earn a maximum of 100 points. A perfect 100 would be reserved for those learners who master advanced content across the board. A standard diploma, however, could be granted to students who earn 70 points or above and master, at a minimum, basic material in each subject area — but no less than proficient material in mathematics, science, history and language arts. To earn the 70 points, the student who makes it only to the basic level in some courses would have to make advanced or honors in other classes. Under such a system, diplomas could be granted to students who are proficient in all subjects or to students who are minimally competent in, say, health and physical education and technology (basic level for 12 points) — as long as they are "whizzes" in other fields, such as foreign language, geography and music (advanced level for 30 points), and proficient in reading, writing, mathematics, history and science (32 points). Something to ponder. The beauty in such a system is that it accommodates differences in children while expecting everyone to function at high levels.

Employers and colleges hold the key to making the academic decathlon system work. If employers and colleges make it clear that they will review students' records and give preference to students who earn advanced diplomas, students will make a goal of earning the advanced diploma.

# HOLDING YOUR FEET TO THE FIRE

## School and District Accountability

Without clear goals and reliable feedback — which is how most school systems operate — it is impossible for them to know if they are headed in the right direction and whether, or how, to adjust programs and policies. Rather than continue to measure success by what goes into schools — the number of books, per-pupil expenditures and teaching ratios — districts need to identify school results with a set of performance measures. Shifting the focus to the efficacy of school efforts means judging schools by the quality of their results, such as student competency over challenging subject matter, enrollments in demanding classes, low suspension and expulsion rates, and high attendance and graduation rates.

## SET CHALLENGING GOALS

Performance measures document individual accomplishment, gauge school and district effectiveness, and lay out plainly the expectations between schools and students. They set the destination and provide the road map to get there. In effect, performance measures serve as mileposts on a long journey, allowing communities to check how far they've traveled and how far they have yet to go. Annually, communities can review the school district's progress and judge its effectiveness. While performance measures, or outputs, are more difficult to measure than school resources, or inputs, they are worth every ounce of effort. As performance targets are set, they are likely to be met.

### Set Long-Term Goals

Setting goals is the chance for the community and district to say where they want the system to be. The comprehensive academic analysis will state in precise terms where the system is on a range of indicators. Goal-setting has three steps:

*   Translate the system mission and vision statement into a set of measurable, long-range improvement goals around which the system and its distinct components can organize.

*   Set a series of annual benchmarks for the district as a whole.

AT A GLANCE

*   **Set challenging goals**

*   **Evaluate principals**

*   **Two principals speak**

*   **Evaluate teachers**

*   **Evaluate superintendents**

*   **Assess customer satisfaction**

*   **Publicize goals and results**

- Strike a deal with staffs from each school at the beginning of the school year about what they will contribute to the system effort to meet annual district targets in the short run and the improvement goals in the long run.

For the effort to be taken seriously, goals should be specific, achievable and results-oriented. Make them simple but ambitious. Selecting multi-year goals of five years or more enables districts to think big, expect more and organize for change.

What's worth tracking? The simple answer is all the indicators measured by your academic analysis. As they are worth measuring, they are also worth tracking. While not all are conducive to system goals, most are. For each indicator, targets should be set for the district as a whole and for specific groups of students. What follows are indicators tracked by **Charlotte-Mecklenburg, NC**.

- The percent of students in the primary years who demonstrate their readiness to begin work in the next grade.

- The percent of middle and high school students who are enrolled in foreign language courses, geometry, algebra and higher-level science courses such as chemistry and physics. (Set separate targets for each.)

- The percent of students taking **Advanced Placement** (AP) courses and exams.

- The percent of students who pass state end-of-course achievement tests at each grade level.

- The percent of students who are deemed "proficient" on state basic minimum skills tests at certain grade levels.

- The percent of students who take the Preliminary Scholastic Assessment Test (PSAT), Scholastic Assessment Test (SAT), American College Testing (ACT) and AP tests as well as increases in the scores.

- At selected grade levels, the percent of students scoring in the top 25 percent nationally on norm-referenced tests and the increases in the average percentile scores.

- The percent of students who are absent.

- The percent of students suspended from school because of minor rule infractions.

**FOR THE EFFORT TO BE TAKEN SERIOUSLY, GOALS SHOULD BE SPECIFIC, ACHIEVABLE AND RESULTS-ORIENTED.**

*For more on goal-setting, see Step 1.*

*Step 3 describes goals and indicators that are worth monitoring.*

- The percent of students expelled from school because of extreme rule infractions.

- The percent of students who drop out of school.

- The gaps in achievement between white and minority students and for other specific groups of students, such as those whose native language is not English or those living in poverty, shown by the data to be lagging behind.

Setting goals is not an exact science. The secret is to shoot high while remaining realistic. Base goals on the data. Go back to the academic analysis to determine, in quantifiable terms, just where you stand with any particular target. For example, setting a goal that states, "One hundred percent of students who enter high school will graduate," is admirable but unlikely to be achieved if your graduation rate hovers around 75 percent. A more reasonable — yet still challenging — increment of gain would be 85 percent. The same analysis should be applied to every outcome worth measuring.

## Set Annual District Benchmarks

Once you've settled on long-term goals, figure out how much you can bite off annually. It may be as easy as dividing your targets by five or whatever long-term goal increment you have settled on. In other words, if you want the percentile ranking on a norm-referenced test to go up 25 points in five years, you might set annual targets of 5 percentile points per year. Or you might challenge your district to start slow but keep improving: 3 points in year one, 4 points in year two and so on. Close analysis by people who know instructional programs well makes sense here.

## Set Annual School Benchmarks

With district goals in place, turn your attention to what schools contribute — what value they add — to students' learning. For each school, that means setting improvement goals customized to its circumstances. Rather than absolute standards, which would require all schools to meet fixed, predetermined objectives, each school competes against itself. A school in distress, for instance, would not be expected to meet overnight the standards of a school that has a history of high academic achievement. This customization protects the integrity of the goal-setting process and keeps everyone challenged:

Low-performing schools and the principals who run them do not feel like the deck is stacked. Schools at the higher end can't afford to sit back in smug satisfaction either. Regardless of their starting point, schools are expected to show significant improvement. Schools that are further behind — those with larger populations of low achievers as part of their baseline data — are expected to make the greater gains because they have the farthest to go to meet the district goals. Maintenance-of-effort goals are established for schools whose achievement levels have topped out.

Set goals for an entire school to encourage collaboration among all facets of a school community. As students move to other schools, delete their records and factor them into the baseline of their new schools. This is a good way to take into account the mobility that occurs inside districts and takes away a prime excuse for poor student performance.

For fairness, make special considerations for schools that serve students with education handicaps, limited English proficiency and those who move frequently. To ensure reliable results, students need to be enrolled at a school for at least 100 days. Don't count suspensions and expulsions in the absenteeism figures. Consider making allowances for some special education students in attendance and academic achievement.

### Different Schools, Different Benchmarks

Consider a district goal for the percent of students in the primary years who demonstrate their readiness to begin work in the next grade. These are indicative of how **Charlotte-Mecklenburg, NC**, structured theirs.

- In School A, 50 percent of first graders are ready for second-grade work. School A may be asked to reduce the percent who are not ready by 30 percent, increasing the share of first graders ready for second-grade work to 65 percent.

- In School B, 70 percent of first graders are ready for second-grade work. School B may be asked to reduce the percent not ready by 20 percent, increasing the share of first graders ready for second-grade work to 76 percent.

- In School C, 85 percent of first graders are ready for second-grade work. School C may be asked to reduce the percent not ready by 10 percent, increasing the share of first graders ready for second-grade work to 87 percent.

The idea is to look at each school's particular baseline and then set challenging but realistic goals each year. Continuous improvement should be expected from all schools, every year.

## Close Gaps Between White and Minority Students

To encourage schools to address achievement gaps between black or white students, rich or poor students, or between the sexes, setting separate sub-goals in each of the student achievement and participation areas is imperative. In other words, if you have goals to reduce suspensions, increase enrollments in higher-level courses and increase the pass rate on end-of-course tests, also set sub-goals that address expectations for specific groups of students shown by the data to be lagging behind the others. Failures of some are masked easily by reviewing results for all students in combination.

*Education Watch: The 1996 State and National Data Book*, published by the **Education Trust**, reveals troubling trends in minority achievement and equity. For instance:

- Between 1970 and 1988, the gap between test scores of minorities and whites was cut in half, but since 1988 the gap has begun to widen again.

- In schools where more than 30 percent of the students are poor, 59 percent of teachers report that they lack sufficient books and other reading resources. Only 16 percent of teachers in more affluent schools report such shortages.

- Poor and minority students are more likely to be taught a low-level curriculum with low standards for performance. Only one in four students from low-income families is placed in a college-preparatory sequence of courses. Poor and minority students are overrepresented in less-challenging general and vocational education programs.

- Roughly 55 of every 100 white and Asian-American students complete algebra II and geometry. Only 35 percent of African-American and Native American seniors take this course sequence. Although one of every four white seniors takes physics, only one in six black seniors, and one in seven Latino seniors, takes this course.

**CONTINUOUS IMPROVEMENT SHOULD BE EXPECTED FROM ALL SCHOOLS, EVERY YEAR.**

### Tie Evaluations to the Goals

America's public schools have evaluation and reward systems precisely backward. The best school employees are paid the same as the worst. Whether you do a good job educating or a bad job, you are treated the same. Staff members aren't paid for excellence. They get raises for time spent on the job, for acquiring extra degrees and for moving into administrative jobs. Job performance is irrelevant.

In most districts, the "old boy network" has a firm grip on the evaluation system. From a few personal snapshots, central office managers determine whether principals are making the grade. They define competence by a checklist of process, administrative trivia and personality traits. Rewards go to staff members who follow the rules. Few incentives urge risk-taking, improved schooling or high academic outcomes for students.

Not paying for performance penalizes the high achiever and rewards the low achiever. To be effective, inducements for change, honors and rewards must be fair, clear and tied to specific results. People respond to incentives — whether they come in the form of dollars, stature or recognition. What gets measured gets done. What gets rewarded gets emphasized. School personnel are no different.

## SETTING GOALS, REWARDING PERFORMANCE

Goals set, goals met: Almost to a person in **Beaufort County, SC**, everyone has stepped up his or her performance, says Superintendent Herman Gaither. People who were settling for mediocre have raised the ceiling. People who were lazy have found new energy. The standards have been set. Every July, Gaither sits with each principal, reviews that school's data and sets expectations for the school. The principal puts together a plan for meeting the expectations. The superintendent and principal meet quarterly to review progress.

Rewarding performance is important in Beaufort — and money isn't the only motivator. Time, title and authority are effective rewards as well. For example, excellent teachers can be rewarded with the title of "master teacher" or "lead teacher"; with the authority of "team leader," "small learning community coordinator" or "department head"; or with extra time for planning.

Tie your evaluation systems directly to the goals established for the district and individual schools. Reward staffs when they succeed, help them shape up when they falter and replace them when they fail. The point is not to single out winners and losers but to create powerful incentives for improvement and positive, demonstrable results. Consider giving bonus checks to principals and school staffs who meet specified student achievement benchmarks. Allowing an entire school to benefit promotes *esprit de corps*. Good teachers have an incentive to help poorer ones. Poorer ones want to be better because rewards depend on performance. Principals visit classrooms to help teachers make the grade.

If you need further convincing, consider a recent study of 16 Kentucky schools involved in the state's landmark 1990 state-wide accountability program. Researcher Carolyn Kelley, an assistant professor of educational administration and a member of the multi-university Consortium for Policy Research in Education, found the combination of rewards (in the form of extra cash or professional pride) and sanctions (in the form of loss of autonomy or bad press) to be a powerful motivator. Uniting those consequences with special help for troubled schools is producing results.

## EVALUATE PRINCIPALS

Author Susan Pimentel and Superintendent John Murphy designed a modern, results-oriented principal evaluation tool for **Charlotte-Mecklenburg, NC**, that measures effectiveness, charts progress, targets areas of need, rewards excellence and ensures that principals get the assistance and support they need to meet expectations. The evaluation tool is among the most inventive in the nation, in large part because it flies in the face of conventional management theory. With 118 schools, most management theorists would argue that the span of control is too broad to permit individual reviews of principal behavior and performance by a single administrator; the superintendent would have to delegate to area superintendents. Not so, Murphy argued. His job was to oversee academic performance district-wide, and his frontline troops in the battle were his building principals. Lose contact with them, Murphy reasoned, and you've lost contact with the education enterprise itself.

REWARD STAFFS WHEN THEY SUCCEED, HELP THEM SHAPE UP WHEN THEY FALTER AND REPLACE THEM WHEN THEY FAIL.

The solution was to design a principal evaluation format that was performance-based and objectively scored, one that relied heavily on parent and community input and one that enjoyed the confidence of the principals. Student achievement got top billing, and achievement measures served as the driving force. Results on such evaluations have nothing to do with personalities and everything to do with performance.

> **➤ An article by Susan Pimentel and John Murphy in *Phi Delta Kappan* on the principal evaluation tool**

## A 100-Point System

In **Charlotte-Mecklenburg, NC**, Murphy and Pimentel developed a scoring rubric that took into account everything from teachers' and parents' views of the principal's leadership to student test scores. The plan gives heavy emphasis to student achievement data and the extent to which district benchmark goals are met (40 points for annual school goals). Results from teacher, parent and student surveys regarding the principal's performance make up the bulk of the rest of the points (20 points from teachers, 20 points from parents, 10 points from students). The better the improvement in scores, the more points the principal earns.

The new system tracks the factors that exemplify schools of exceptional quality, such as student competency over challenging subject matter, enrollment in demanding classes, test scores, suspension and expulsion rates, absenteeism, school completion and college acceptance rates. Test scores and class participation data disaggregated by race, ethnicity and socio-economic status, along with the opinions of teachers, students and parents, measure the strength of the instructional program and students' academic progress. To top it off, facility reports, financial and program audits, data on personnel management and other information collected at the central office level are worth 10 points.

Perhaps most important in a reform environment, Murphy could award bonus points to principals who were in special circumstances (restoring a failing school, trying an innovation and the like). In short, innovators and troubleshooters would not be penalized. Low scores, for example, may be the result of having to push through school reforms with a staff used to doing things their own way. The principal is placed on notice by the results but not penalized — at least not initially. He or she has a year to attend to the low teacher morale. This process puts a human face on an otherwise exacting system.

## Focus on Clients

Under conventional evaluation systems, principals tend to worry most about pleasing central office administrators, the people upon whom their jobs most depend. Students, parents and teachers take a back seat. **Charlotte-Mecklenburg, NC's** new system refocused principal attention. Parents, teachers and students regularly appraised the performance of school administrators. Their views were surveyed annually, and their responses were factored into the evaluation process. Principals got points for satisfying client groups in areas of safety and discipline, home/school connections, and instructional and administrative leadership. Parents, teachers and students had the opportunity to "tell it like it is" without fear of retribution. There was safety — and fairness — in numbers; the new system exchanged the opinion of one evaluator from the central office (who visited the school only occasionally) for the views of many who worked in the school day in and day out.

We have found no substitute for giving the consumer direct access to the supplier. Once they take on the role of evaluator, parents and students move from the sidelines into the heart of the learning enterprise to share responsibility for improving education. Surveys make partners of parents and students and help balance the relationship, administrator to teacher. Moreover, sustained improvement is unlikely if a principal does it in isolation, without the cooperation of teachers or, worse yet, "on the backs" of teachers. Thus, canvassing teachers' views does more than boost morale. It provides principals with crucial feedback. No more top-down system — administrators evaluate teachers, and teachers, in turn, evaluate principals. Under such a system, Charlotte's principals can lose their jobs if they don't take proper care.

## Ratings and Consequences

In this setting, every single principal in the district reported directly to Murphy — all 118. Each one was individually rated, and the scores fell across four broad ranges; the best got high ratings and required little or no follow-up; a majority received acceptable ratings and required modest follow-up; a sizable minority received "needs help" and got it; a small number were put on notice.

SURVEYS MAKE PARTNERS OF PARENTS AND STUDENTS AND HELP BALANCE THE RELATIONSHIP, ADMINISTRATOR TO TEACHER.

THE EXPECTATIONS
WERE CLEAR:
EVERY ADULT
IN THE SYSTEM
WAS EXPECTED
TO IMPROVE
STUDENT RESULTS.

To be rated "stellar" or "above standard," principals had to amass high point totals. And they needed to earn at least half of the points available in the benchmark goal area and client survey areas; these minimums ensured that principals could not court parents, teachers and students and fail to attend to student achievement or attend to student achievement while ignoring parents, teachers and students. Different consequences attached to the results. "Good" principals breathed easy. Principals who received either a "stellar" or an "above standard" rating were exempt from evaluation the next year as long as they maintained their benchmark achievement levels within 10 percent. How they choose to get the job done was up to them — no more looking over their shoulders, no more interference from central managers — as long as their means to success were moral, legal and ethical.

For **Charlotte-Mecklenburg, NC**, principals who ranked "at standard" or "below standard," the story changed. They could not escape attention or intervention. Improvement plans were put quickly into motion; the assistance included practical advice from the superintendent himself. Principals rated "below standard" had to improve in one year or face reassignment. No time was wasted. Children's futures depend on the skill and competence of the school's instructional leader.

One principal said, "When Superintendent Murphy first came here, I felt safe because I knew there were at least 30 principals who were worse than me. Now I'm really worried." In four years, 35 principals were dismissed for poor performance. The expectations were clear: Every adult in the system was expected to improve student results. For the sake of the principals and the children, action was swift. We help no one by taking years to show a person to the door.

The single exception to the new results-oriented evaluation tool was new principals. (It takes time — a couple of years at least — for a principal's leadership to take hold.) What was important was that new principals developed an environment conducive to high levels of student achievement, so that was what was measured. In the years thereafter, hard evidence of student achievement and teacher, parent and student satisfaction became the measures.

➤ **Competency evaluation components**

## TWO PRINCIPALS SPEAK

Addie Moore and Fred Slade, **Charlotte-Mecklenburg, NC**, principals with more than five decades of experience between them, came up through the education ranks at a time when a good principal was preoccupied with books, buildings, buses and budgets at the expense of education vision and outcomes. Both had to retool in the era of Superintendent John Murphy. Representative of many others in the schools, both turned troubled inductions into leading administrations in just a few years. The recipe for success is as simple as one part sound evaluation, one part targeted training and one part willingness to change.

### FOCUSED ON THE RIGHT STUFF

### Principal Addie Moore, Pinewood Elementary School

*"On a scale of one to 10, administrators and teachers were flying high, rated at the top end of the scale while student achievement hovered around the low end, in the one- or two-point range. It didn't make sense. The evaluation system of years past was a mere checklist designed to make everybody feel good, but it did next to nothing to improve student achievement," says Moore.*

*When the new evaluation system was put into effect, Moore was principal at Pinewood. By her own admission, her evaluation was not as high as she wanted it to be. "The new evaluation system, with student achievement as its centerpiece, was a wake-up call that I needed to do some changing. It made me ask, 'How flexible am I? Am I listening enough? What kind of support do I need?' It wasn't just about what the system had to do anymore. The evaluation system got me and my staff focused on the right stuff."*

*Her assessment was precise. It told the story and pinpointed the problems: Student achievement was low and flat almost across the board. Attendance was abysmal.*

*Absenteeism among black students was double that among white students. Teachers complained that they had little input, that their opinions were not valued. Parents said they weren't getting enough information about the instructional progress of their children. Students objected to the many interruptions during the day.*

*Armed with pages of disaggregated data, detailed survey analyses and pointed warnings contained within the evaluation's summary comments, Moore set out to attack every deficiency. "I took a yellow marker and highlighted all the inadequacies noted in the evaluation, whether they came in the form of academic data or survey critiques. The shortcomings became my priorities for the next year. I sat with my teachers and together we crafted our plan of attack. Then I asked for help from the superintendent and my executive director. Unlike years past, when training was developed in a vacuum and dispensed to me in a take-it-or-leave-it fashion, someone actually asked me what I needed and developed training to meet that need. That's different — totally different. And look where we are today!"*

*In two short years, Pinewood went from a school that had never achieved its goals during Moore's tenure to a school achieving 95 out of 100 of its benchmark goal points, registering the highest point totals in the system. "I established a strong instructional monitoring system, which gets me into classrooms every single day for hours at a time. Don't look for me between the hours of 9 a.m. and 11 a.m. That's when I observe teachers, no excuse. In conjunction with this effort, we began to closely track individual student progress at Pinewood and meet regularly in teams to discuss, by name, any student not making the grade. We ask ourselves what we aren't doing. For example, a couple of years ago, we marshaled our resources to extend the day for those who weren't succeeding. Our instincts were right, some students just took longer to learn the same things. We didn't stop there. Teacher teams sprung up in response to the call for more of a say-so about school affairs. Regular progress reports to parents became a top priority. Attendance was attacked with a vengeance. We confined intercom announcements to the morning, before class. No more interruptions, just as students had requested. We changed from top to bottom."*

*Moore has the results to prove it: She received the honored "stellar" rating on the 1995 evaluation. Modestly, Moore claims, "If the evaluation system worked for me, it can work for anybody. The system is fair. It's not a game of 'gotcha.' I know up front what's expected of me and everywhere I turn, there is support to help me improve."*

## ACCOUNTABILITY, NOT MICROMANAGEMENT

### Principal Fred Slade, Reedy Creek Elementary School

*Fred Slade faced similar challenges. Trained as a secondary school administrator, Slade by his own admission had a firm grip on how to manage a building, but didn't know the first thing about elementary curriculum and the best way to deliver it. In 1993 and 1994, Reedy Creek Elementary School failed to meet its benchmark goals.*

Problems were cited in all key subject areas, including reading, writing, mathematics and science. Students themselves were calling for tougher standards and more rigorous study. Too few felt challenged. School pride was gone; on the survey, a majority of students said they'd rather go to another school. Teachers complained about the lack of open and shared leadership. Student discipline also was a concern.

Today, Reedy Creek basks in the light of renewed public confidence: In 1995, the school made its benchmark goals, registering a 17-point gain. The teacher, parent and student surveys noted improvement in all areas. Members of the school family who once felt disenfranchised now feel welcomed, supported and safe at Reedy Creek. All agree, Reedy Creek is an inviting place to learn and to teach, marked by harmony and a common sense of purpose.

What made the difference? Slade cites the new evaluation system. "For the first time, I got frank and honest feedback. There's no beating around the bush with the new system. How much and how well my students are learning is tracked closely. I hear directly from parents, students and teachers — not in an ad hoc fashion but in an organized and uniform manner via the surveys. I wanted to know what I needed to do, to do what I do better. The evaluation told me exactly that. It gave me the blueprint."

Tracing his progress, Slade notes that he had no choice but to shift his focus to outcomes. "We began each day by asking ourselves: 'Why are we doing what we are doing? What are children going to get from this?' If the answer was 'Nothing,' we moved on to something else. I got myself out of the office and into classrooms. Understand, I wasn't being told how to get the job done. The superintendent had clearly passed the baton to me and others in the principal ranks to take our authority.

"Accountability, not micromanagement, was the name of the game. And the help was there to make the shift. For the first time I was asked what training I needed. Along with my input, people looked at my data and designed a suitable course of study for me. I can't think of a time over the past three years I attended a training session and felt it was a waste of my time or not relevant. I took advantage of every possible opportunity and continue to do so. In a process similar to the reteaching loop we have instituted for our students, our progress is monitored closely, our weaknesses and strengths exposed, and targeted training supplied. Then we are assessed again for one reason and one reason only: so we can get better."

## EVALUATE TEACHERS

Results-based principal evaluation systems have many implications — and hold big promise — for teachers. They point up the need to turn teacher evaluation systems inside out by reducing reliance on checklists filled out after a one-hour visit to a classroom and instead embracing a portfolio of performance. A fair and effective evaluation system discriminates between effective and ineffective teaching, gives teachers tools to improve, is results-based and allows for some peer review. In that vein, we recommend a system that determines the extent to which:

- teachers are implementing the system's teaching and learning program,

- optimal conditions for learning are created and

- academic benchmark goals are achieved.

To capture the depth and richness of teachers' performances, consider building a portfolio — electronic if you have the resources — complete with analyses of student achievement data; detailed feedback from a multitude of observations; and examples of model lessons, students' work or any other items that teachers feel best exemplify their daily performance.

Such a system would require sitting down with each teacher at the beginning of each school year and, against the backdrop of school benchmarks, negotiating realistic but challenging achievement goals. Goals could include scores on end-of-course tests, percent of students prepared for work at the next grade level, mastery of curriculum objectives or the full range of student participation goals. Rather than absolute standards, which require all teachers to meet fixed, predetermined objectives, the challenge is to set improvement goals and ask teachers to compete against themselves. Goals should be tailor-made to a teacher's specific population of students.

What about asking teachers to observe the performance of their peers? Varied perspectives could provide teachers with more frequent and meaningful feedback on practice. Observations from students in the higher grades could be factored into the mix as well. Any good student can tell you which teachers are tough, interesting, interested and well prepared.

Teaching is a complex process, and any attempt to define it must include a full range of pertinent criteria. The principal, or other person or persons responsible for teacher evaluations, should focus on the presence of instructional elements and practices that are documented by sound research and experience to make a difference. **E.D. Hirsch** does an excellent review of the literature in his new book, *The Schools We Need and Why We Don't Have Them*, and demonstrates the congruence among dozens of national and international studies. The most salient points of agreement among researchers are that effective teachers:

- Start with a brief statement of goals.

- Connect new lessons to previous knowledge.

- Sustain focus on content.

- Maintain clarity and detail in presentation.

- Deliver coherent, thorough lessons with few shifts in topics.

- Use whole-class instruction most of the time, obtaining responses and checks for understanding from each student.

- Call on students regularly.

- Ask higher-level questions that require more than a "yes" or "no."

- Introduce material at a steady pace in small, easily mastered steps.

- Use review and repetition but not incessantly.

- Use seatwork sparingly or in short, frequent bursts, alternating between discussing problems and allowing children to work with problems on their own.

- Provide regular, quick and nonevaluative feedback to students.

- Convey high expectations.

- Maintain a warm, supportive yet businesslike atmosphere.

- End with a class summary of where the lesson went and what it did, like good storytellers.

However the system is configured, involving teachers in developing, testing and monitoring any new process makes sense. Common agreement and understanding will go a long way to building a credible system.

> **Indicators of good practice for teacher evaluation**

ANY GOOD STUDENT CAN TELL YOU WHICH TEACHERS ARE TOUGH, INTERESTING, INTERESTED AND WELL PREPARED.

# EVALUATE SUPERINTENDENTS

Achieving and sustaining high-quality schooling call for a wide range of leadership, supervisory and administrative competencies. The bottom line, however, is student results. Like the principal and teacher evaluation tools, superintendent evaluations need to do more than measure the presence or absence of particular practices and competencies. Instead they must tie practice to desired results. In this way, factors that exemplify a district of exceptional quality can be tracked through objective sources of information, such as student participation and achievement data; staff, parent and student attitudes; financial, facility and program audits; editorial comment and criticism; school visits, staff meetings and community appearances; and school/university/business collaborations.

Mirroring the principal evaluation system, consider adopting a 100-point system that heavily emphasizes student achievement data. For instance, reserve 40 points for benchmark goal attainment and progress on other student achievement fronts. Specifically, focus on the extent to which:

- district and school benchmark goals are met

- the performance of lower-performing students improves

- the performance of traditionally low-performing schools improves

- the district makes progress on state and national assessments for all segments of the student population

Use the remaining 60 points to measure the extent to which the superintendent demonstrates leadership in four key areas:

- **Organizational management:** the ability to develop a collective district vision and formulate strategic plans, goals and change efforts that serve the education needs of all students.

- **Instructional leadership:** the ability to assess the education condition of the system, to guide the staff and community in determining instructional goals for the future and to put in place a long-range plan that will ensure goals are attained within a specified time.

- **Executive leadership:** the ability to run a finely tuned business enterprise similar to that of chief executive officers of major corporations.

- **Communications/community–district relations:** the ability to communicate the school system's mission, goals, programs and requirements to everyone directly involved with the system and the wider public.

An additional 10 points for "special initiative" or extra credit could be available for the board for extraordinary innovation or progress. Rewarding a superintendent for bold and courageous innovations is important to make sure that the superintendent is not penalized for reform initiatives. The superintendent can provide the board with a portfolio of supporting documentation that might include such things as awards and honors, creative school/university/business collaborations and reports of other innovations.

## ASSESS CUSTOMER SATISFACTION

District personnel and principals who are launching a school improvement effort will be much better equipped to move forward if they know what their constituencies — teachers, parents and students — are thinking. Do all three groups think school discipline is well in hand? Is everyone clear on what the academic standards are? Are people's attitudes positive or negative? Customer satisfaction surveys are useful tools to get people talking. They signal a system's determination to listen and respond to more than a select few; they make everyone a part of the improvement effort even if they don't have the time to be part of a decision-making team.

Surveys also can secure valuable information about your parent community: income and education levels, expectations for students, the number of student working hours per week, the number of student TV viewing hours per week and the average number of hours spent on homework per night. They provide the opportunity to learn about how much parents participate in the education of their child. Do they participate in teacher conferences? In the PTA? How often do they volunteer at school? Attend school programs or events? How often do they assist their children with homework? Visit classrooms? That kind of information can help to tailor a social covenant governing what the communities expect of the schools and what schools expect of the community and students.

Asking teachers what they think reflects the reality that sustained school improvement is unlikely if teachers don't feel respected or if morale is low.

**CUSTOMER SATISFACTION SURVEYS ARE USEFUL TOOLS TO GET PEOPLE TALKING.**

The sooner you attempt this venture, the sooner you are able to establish a baseline of parent, student and teacher attitudes, so progress can be tracked year to year. After the initial survey, annually monitoring opinions gives you information about trends and what the system and individual schools need to address. It differs by school.

One of the easiest ways to get the surveys out and back again is to put individual schools in charge of the effort. Creating incentives for high returns — which could come in the form of awards or points on an evaluation system — makes good sense. For ease of scoring and analyzing results, make sure your surveys can be scored by a machine. To give the surveys weight, develop a district profile, separate school profiles and compare the results of one to the others. Is the school performing above the district averages? Below? In what areas? Are the trends good?

➤ **The right questions for teachers, parents and students**

## PUBLICIZE GOALS AND RESULTS

The final step is to broadcast the goals and results for all to see. Most districts collect a wealth of useful information, but there is a dearth of it available to the public. Parents and the broader community know only in vague terms whether or not they like their local schools. Most do not know how their schools stack up in the district, the state or the nation. Annual school reports enable parents to link their child's individual performance to system goals and judge the progress of their child's school against other schools in meeting goals. In addition, individual school staffs can compare system-wide results with their schools' results and, where weaknesses are identified, take appropriate remedial action.

So too, the central office staff can use the information to identify system strengths and weaknesses, compare and contrast different school programs, and allocate resources and special assistance accordingly. Moreover, community members, who are owed an accounting for the investment they make in local education, can track the progress of schools and make sensible decisions about how their money is being spent. Regular and accurate reports to the public hold staffs' feet to the fire. Taxpayers pay attention. They demand excellence.

Regular reports have major implications for students, parents and members of the broader community. Only informed participants can make accurate judgments and support suitable corrective steps. As indicators of progress, carefully designed and executed reports give systems backbone.

> ➤ **Samples of school annual report cards**

## Focus on Student Performance

Achievement data is the heart and soul of any report. Results should be disaggregated by race and sex, comparing the district to the state and the nation and noting progress over time. With achievement tests, be sure to display the absolute score, the gain achieved from the prior year and the size of any gaps in achievement. In addition, include data on student participation, attendance, absenteeism, course enrollments, retentions, suspensions and dropouts. Track students by race and sex, and compare the data to district percentages. Demonstrating progress over time serves to strengthen reports.

## Report Other Indicators and Information

Each school should have an individual booklet so that every parent and teacher can have a copy. Along with current scores and percentages on a

**REGULAR AND ACCURATE REPORTS TO THE PUBLIC HOLD STAFFS' FEET TO THE FIRE.**

---

### IN BEAUFORT

# I'D RATHER DO IT MY WAY

Using the tried-and-true, 19-member committee approach that had worked so well in setting standards, **Beaufort County, SC**, established a "school report card committee." The central office staffed the committee, made up of principals, teachers, students, parents and community members, with the district's data analyst, Catherine McCaslin. She knew what data was available, where it was, what shape it was in and how to get it.

The committee met a number of times to hammer out the common elements of the format and contents. Members immediately recognized that the document had to be brisk and informative, but sample report cards from around the country seemed dull, repetitive and uninteresting. They decided that each Beaufort report card would be the same size and contain a common core of data to permit easy and informed comparison, school to school, but that each would have some "uncommon" information as well. First, each report would have a distinctive cover (each would include the school name and a Beaufort reference), and each would use its own art. Second, each report would contain a message from the principal outlining what's special about the school, where it's going and so on.

range of indicators, include the list of long-term goals and an explanation of how scores are calculated. Keep your audience in mind. Parents and members of the broader community, who may not have the expertise of educators, will be reviewing the results. Display the information creatively, using simple graphs wherever possible. To highlight school initiatives and unique endeavors, insert special commentary. Invite your local newspapers to publish the report cards. Most are glad to oblige.

**Charlotte-Mecklenburg, NC**, published an annual report as a special supplement to *The Charlotte Observer*. The data compares each school to its annual goals, to the district average and to state and national averages on a wide range of indicators, from SAT scores to the number of minority students passing **Advanced Placement** exams.

Consider incorporating a series of profiles within the annual reports. School, student and staff profiles give the reader a context in which to consider the results and give individual schools the opportunity to differentiate themselves from the pack. Schools can showcase their innovations and play to the imagination of the public. Student profiles can include such characteristics as the number of students in each grade, the number and kind of exceptional children, the ethnic diversity and sex of the student body, the turnover rate, the number of limited English proficiency students and the number of students on free or reduced price lunch. (None should be used as an excuse for poor performance, however.) A breakdown of number and kind of staff positions, teachers' years of experience and their degrees are examples of information that parents want and deserve to have.

School reports also can document resource needs. Most districts institute change incrementally because they lack funds to do otherwise. As you pilot new ideas, such as computers in classrooms or a school dedicated to the arts or the sciences, publicize the efforts. What is the ratio of students to librarians, students to counselors, students to parent liaisons? How about the ratio of students to computers? Are media resources and science labs up to date? Does the school have a parent resource center? How many Advanced Placement courses does the school offer? Does the school have interactive TV capacity? In the long run, taxpayers may support increased school spending for targeted reasons so long as results are forthcoming. When taxpayers know that some schools have access to certain resources, they may apply pressure to provide the same resources to all schools and take up the banner for bond initiatives.

# SO WHAT'S IN IT FOR ME?

## Developing New Partnerships

Education reform cannot happen without a new level of involvement by friends of the schools: parents, business people, religious and civic leaders, and citizens. In **Step 1**, community members help position school issues within the broader framework of the community's overall well-being. In **Step 2**, community members help set standards. In **Step 3**, community members help frame questions and can even call on the schools for specific academic reports. And while **Step 4** emphasizes what goes on in schools, community support for change is critical. So too, **Steps 5 and 6** — student and district accountability — do not work without broadly based community support.

### CHALLENGE YOUR COMMUNITY

#### Issue a Call to Arms

Telling the truth about the state of the schools is a defining moment in a district's life. It is well suited to a back-to-school rally. Convene the community — educators, parents, students, business and political leaders, and taxpayers — to hear it like it is and as it will be. Issue a call to arms. Invite people to gather together to come to grips with the realities of schooling. Find a space large enough to hold the school community. <u>Charlotte-Mecklenburg, NC</u>, rented the convention center, for instance, and the strategy galvanized the community.

### AT A GLANCE

- Challenge your community

- Involve the community in new ways

- Involve parents in new ways

- Involve businesses in new ways

- Use the media and other tools

---

## IN CHARLOTTE-MECKLENBURG

### WORDS TO MOVE MEN'S MINDS

When John Murphy became superintendent in <u>Charlotte-Mecklenburg, NC</u>, he held a small back-to-school meeting: He invited everyone in the district to come to the coliseum. Ten thousand people showed up, among them most of the district's teachers and administrators and hundreds of eager citizens, wearing T-shirts Murphy had issued. On the front: "The greatest risk is not running one." On the back: "Join the conspiracy to reform our schools or we'll hold the revolution without you."

*Step 3 provides the data and analyses for these community conversations.*

Telling the simple truth without softening the blow takes fortitude. It means exposing weaknesses as well as strengths, but the payoff is big. Every revolution needs a catalyst to release the seeds of discontent. The academic inventory outlined in Step 3 can serve as yours. Information is power. It makes equals out of people — and that fact is not lost on your community partners. Remember, too, all school systems are in the same boat.

## Keep the Message Upbeat but Do Not Mince Words

Speak of your hopes, expectations, plans and concerns. Celebrate your accomplishments just as you reveal your flaws. Let the community know that you plan to set system goals — ambitious ones that target current weaknesses and cause teachers and students to stretch. Let your audience know that you will report regularly and honestly on progress. Everyone can keep track of how well the school system is doing.

Both Herman Gaither, **Beaufort County, SC**, superintendent, and John Murphy, **Charlotte-Mecklenburg, NC**, superintendent, emphasize the importance of "coming clean" with your community. People won't believe you, join you or stick with you when the going gets tough if you don't admit to problems and ask for help. Frame the message positively. Gaither adds: "We are doing well — but we can do a whole lot better, and we intend to."

Remind your school community that reporting gaps in academic performance that may exist between black and white students, rich and poor students, or male and female students is not meant to embarrass or point fingers of blame but to push to improve.

Let staffs know that they have the professional running room they need to get the job done — subject to a simple test: student success. Let them know that the central office is restructuring to provide services to schools, not the other way around.

## Develop a School–Community Compact

The honest exchange about what's good and bad sets the stage for a compact that defines rights and responsibilities: what the community expects from the schools, what the schools expect from the community and what both expect of students.

Why are compacts so important? First, they give the public the opportunity to "recharter" the public schools. Second, they give schools the opportunity to reacquire legitimacy. They set the stage for a community strategy, not a school strategy, for educating every child to high levels. The schools become *their* schools. Reciprocity and mutuality are created. All parties to the compact are stakeholders, and everyone's interests are served by working together. When schools have an explicit mandate, they are more likely to be safe, orderly and excellent.

## INVOLVE THE COMMUNITY IN NEW WAYS

### Take Stock and Involve Everyone

Inventory the education resources in your community. *Is There a Public for Public Schools?* devotes a section to the natural resources in every community. In one way or another, Mathews suggests harnessing the resources of individuals; even those who have little formal instruction may know what makes for excellence in education. Poll citizens at local religious, social and fraternal organizations and community centers. Give them examples of how they can

### IN BEAUFORT

## ONE-ON-ONE TUTORING

Lew Wessel, a youthful retiree to **Beaufort County, SC**, from Washington, DC, has created Operation 100%, an early intervention tutoring program run by volunteers. They read to and with first graders who are behind; their objective is to get each one to grade level by the end of first grade. Each tutor meets with students for half an hour every day, one-on-one.

The program began in Hilton Head Primary, spread to Beaufort Elementary and was to open in September 1997 in M.C. Riley Elementary in Blufton. As imitation is the sincerest form of flattery, Wessel is pleased to report that Operation 100% is now under way in Appleton, WI, as well. The brother of one of the tutors chairs the Appleton School Board and was so impressed with the Beaufort program when he visited that he returned with 12 Appletonians for a closer look. They bought it lock, stock and barrel and now have made it theirs.

Does it work? Hilton Head Primary Principal Julie Grant reports that 80 percent of the children tutored are now on grade level. Moreover, 90 percent of the tutors (mostly retirees) hadn't been in an elementary school since they were students (or parents of students) themselves; today they are not only happy and effective tutors, but they also are advocates for the schools.

help: Quilting can teach geometric and art concepts; cooking can teach science, mathematics and nutrition concepts. Ask citizens to tell you what they do well. Find out whether they've ever taught anybody and whether they are willing to try. Their involvement can reaffirm the importance of public education and increase your capacity to educate many times over.

## Use the Community as a Classroom

Use community organizations to educate. Schools have an opportunity to pattern themselves after the Girl and Boy Scouts where scouts do most of the work under the mindful eyes of parents and members of the community. With community partners, schools can design learning activities that are school-guided, not school-provided.

A zoo's staff can teach from its unique perspective. A television station has creative resources for teaching language arts. A builder can teach about practical uses of geometry and trigonometry. Museums complement history and arts studies. Choirs and orchestras train musicians. The education that is "out

## IN BEAUFORT

## ACADEMIC CHALLENGE

A decade ago, under the leadership of an inventive Beaufort County, SC, high school principal, Steve Ballowe, the Beaufort community began the Academic Challenge. It involves all grade 5–12 schools in the county, public and private. (Two adjoining counties, Jasper and Colleton, also participate.) A recent Academic Challenge was held on the shared campus of Hilton Head High, Hilton Head Elementary, Hilton Head Primary and McCracken Middle schools; extensive facilities were needed to accommodate the more than 2,000 student participants and the faculty, judges, friends and families who joined in.

With all the excitement of an Olympic decathlon or a track-and-field day, the Academic Challenge offers 15 events with first, second and third prizes in each, as well as other award categories to broaden its appeal. The events are spread among the various buildings on the Hilton Head campus. The awards ceremony itself draws thousands on Saturday afternoon, with standing room only in the Hilton Head High School gym.

Not only does the event highlight academic accomplishment and put it on a par with athletics, but it also is a community-building exercise that enjoys broad community and business support. So important is it to the school community that the day itself is a part of the teacher's contract; they are all expected to be there.

there" provides an important point/counterpoint to the education that goes on in schools. Community education can bring learning alive with examples of concepts and skills in practice.

## Celebrate Academics

The community needs to celebrate scholars, to say that solving quadratic equations and reading Shakespeare are more important than blocking on the football team or cheering on the pep squad. No better way to improve schools exists than for the adults in the community to send positive signals. Students make a connection between classwork and the future. Students see that schooling is a tangible investment. "You know you've made it," says Guilford, ME, Superintendent Norm Higgins, "when teachers get the test results and they give each other high fives in the corridors. You know you've made it when students stand and cheer for academic achievement the way they would in the final seconds of a basketball game."

## Involve Community Health and Social Service Agencies

No institution can excel at everything, although schools try. While schools may provide day care, they are not day-care institutions; while they may house service providers, they should not deliver the services firsthand.

As management expert Peter Drucker notes, successful organizations do a few things well. No organization can do many things well; when an organization tries to serve many masters, it sinks to the lowest common denominator. When schools attempt to fill the social services breach single-handedly and try to be all things to all people, they emerge as poor care providers and worse educators.

Make no mistake, schools are a constant in the lives of children and are able to pull many out of desperate circumstances. Indeed, ameliorating children's problems is a matter of self-interest for schools. Hungry, sick and disoriented children do not make good students. But schools should keep their mission front and center, and that mission is teaching and learning. Schools should concentrate their energies on education and outsource other tasks to other institutions.

"YOU KNOW YOU'VE MADE IT WHEN TEACHERS GET THE TEST RESULTS AND THEY GIVE EACH OTHER HIGH FIVES IN THE CORRIDORS."
— Norm Higgins

## THE COALITION FOR GOALS 2000

Groups across your community are succeeding in helping children and families in ways that will amaze you. Someone you know is trying to start a special program or find volunteers to help keep one going; chapters of national organizations are struggling but succeeding at helping adults read or encouraging students to stay in school.

The **Coalition for Goals 2000**, an alliance of 145 national organizations with state and local affiliates — some of them in your hometown — was created to help communities identify and leverage local resources and to provide the information and tools people need to make informed decisions.

As part of a local leadership team, Coalition members, such as nurses who are members of the Association of Women's Health, Obstetrical and Neonatal Nurses, can support and inform local readiness-for-school programs. The Association of Junior Leagues International is engaged with enrichment programs, including before- and after-school programs; First Book provides new books to children without them. Members of the National School Supply and Equipment Association and members of the National Association of Temporary Service and Staffing are small businesses eager to help schools and teachers with curriculum, scholarships and more. Jobs for America's Graduates is helping students train for work while still in school.

The Coalition works to connect people to programs and practices that work through *GOAL LINE* and its ***Raising the Standard*** products and services.

Specifically, schools should:

- Establish links to local community and social service agencies. These agencies often are willing to move their services close to or into schools, where children and families can access them.

- Establish links to senior citizens, retirees and others who normally don't come into contact with the schools. One caring adult can make all the difference to a child's success.

- Establish links to local police departments, which also deal with children's problems when they spill out into streets and homes.

But do not let the academic mission waver or the academic budget hemorrhage.

With few notable exceptions, schools as physical plants remain vastly under-used. Schools are typically open for six hours on weekdays and closed on weekends and during vacations. Schools need to stay open longer, extending the day and year. As Lamar Alexander notes, no business could succeed if it closed its doors at 3 p.m. every afternoon and closed altogether for two and a half months each summer.

As part of the compact, community, social and health agencies need to drop bureaucratic boundaries, inject flexibility into funding streams and stop focusing on narrow service jurisdictions. Schools, for their part, must welcome them as partners. Consolidating the services in a neighborhood school can energize them.

➤ **Information on organizing your community from the National Education Goals Panel**

## IN GUILFORD

## SCHOOL WITHOUT END

Floating in the American subconscious is a sense of school as the center of the community. In part a carry-over from the days in which America was largely rural (as recently as 1900 nearly 50 percent of all Americans lived on farms; today fewer than 3 percent do), it also reflects a romantic view of a more tranquil and pastoral past. But such schools still exist. **Murfreesboro, TN's** Cason Lane Academy with its extended school program is one. **Guilford, ME's** Piscataquis Community High School is another. It is open 12 hours a day (nine hours on Saturday) and serves as a vital community resource.

Not only is significant coursework "beamed in" to Piscataquis High from the University of Maine at Orono (for high school students and adults in the community, including teachers who are earning additional credits), but regular classes also meet after normal school hours. In addition, the high school houses the town library and media center, bringing both hardcover books and the Internet within reach of everyone in the community. Not surprisingly, Guilford residents view the high school as welcoming and interesting.

Is there any more powerful tool for building community support than making schools genuine community institutions? The Guilford example is the norm in many small towns and villages across America and helps explain why the *Phi Delta Kappan*-sponsored Gallup Poll has shown high support for schools in towns and villages across America for the past 25 years. Citizens give these schools As and Bs. Only in our big, anonymous cities do citizens systematically give the schools low marks.

➤ **Resources about community—school partnerships**

# STEP 7

WE NEED TO
GET PARENTS
INTO THE
HEART OF THE
LEARNING
ENTERPRISE
TO SHARE
RESPONSIBILITY
WITH SCHOOLS
FOR HOW WELL
THEIR CHILDREN
LEARN.

## INVOLVE PARENTS IN NEW WAYS

Children need other things in addition to strong academics at school — a healthy start, physical safety, emotional security and involved parents. Three of the best predictors of student success are factors that families control: the loving attention of an adult, daily independent reading and strong values.

Too often, however, parents and family members are relegated to the sidelines of education. Schools need to invest properly in this relationship and stop trying to do everything on their own. Bring parents back to school. They can make your job much easier.

There are many traditional parent activities, including joining the PTA or Booster Club, chaperoning school trips and functions, conferring with teachers and raising money for special events. We do not denigrate those activities; they are compelling, but they do not go far enough. We need to get parents into the heart of the learning enterprise to share responsibility with schools for how well their children learn.

➤ Resources that can help schools involve parents in new ways

### Allow Parental Choice

An essential step to building strong and sustained partnerships with parents is to give them a voice in deciding which school their children attend. The rich have long enjoyed the privilege of selecting the best schools for their children. Extending this option to the general public not only is fair and just, but it also makes schools accountable. And it significantly increases parents' enthusiasm, their willingness to be involved in the life of the school. Choice pushes parental and public involvement to their logical conclusion; it permits parents and the broader community to create the learning communities they seek for their children. Respect flourishes because the relationship is voluntary.

When schools of choice are introduced to a system, all schools become more responsive to their students. They have to vie for customers. Rather than having to "grin and bear it," families can vote with their feet and take their business elsewhere. Without the discipline of competition, organizations — whether in the private or public sector — begin to serve themselves.

Monopolies are insulating and tend to make people lazy. In a choice system, schools must either perform, improve or perish. Choice builds flexibility and responsiveness into the system by changing the locus of control to the customers.

> ➤ **Information from the Center for Education Reform and others interested in charters and choice**

## Make Parents Part of the Governing Team

Only by making concerted efforts to create a shared sense of purpose between parents and staffs can schools reduce the alienation that many children and parents feel, especially the poor and dispossessed. Stark differences in backgrounds and cultures and between teachers and students can create distrust. Teachers often respond by lowering expectations. Children answer back by "acting out." Parents, if they were victims of low expectations themselves, "tune out." On the other hand, asking parents to engage in a dialogue supports cooperation and collaboration. Serving on a school governance team that assesses academic needs, constructs a detailed school plan for improvement and works to develop a more positive school climate reconnects parents to schools.

These are not idle words. Any school incorporating parents on governance teams is flooded with parents. These parents are regulars who assist with the important work of student learning. The payoff is better academic performance and improved student confidence. Schools report higher attendance rates, lower disciplinary referrals and higher test scores — not to mention improved staff morale and parent relations. This improvement paves the way for incentives that encourage parents to be involved with the school on a daily basis, as teachers, volunteers, tutors, mentors and chaperones on school trips.

## Communicate Clearly

The school–parent alliance is strengthened when the academic standards appear in user-friendly brochures. Parents want to know what they can expect their child to learn at every grade, age or performance level. Putting standards in the hands of parents puts them in the driver's seat. Traditional report cards reveal too little.

## READINESS, BIG TIME

Readiness is more than physical maturity. It is a state of mind and a set of activities. Middle-class families take much of it for granted, but there's a lot the schools can do to "broker" readiness activities (without letting their own instructional budget hemorrhage in the process). For example, Superintendent John Murphy used **Charlotte-Mecklenburg, NC's** Interfaith Council as a meeting place, sounding board and resource center to hammer out a community-wide commitment to children's services. Kids who are hungry, tired and frightened don't make super-star students, Murphy reasoned, and he used the resources that the Interfaith Council represented to direct the community's attention to solving the problem. Among other things, the local "Welcome Wagon" that greets newcomers included in its information packet material about the schools and what parents could do to prepare their youngsters. New mothers were visited in the hospital and given not just free paper diapers but also material about the Charlotte-Mecklenburg schools. Preschool PTAs were formed.

Beaufort does much the same with a special flair that is both practical and whimsical. The school district, in partnership with Beaufort Community Hospital, gives every newborn a tiny T-shirt with smiling animals above the following legend:

BORN TO BE LOVED
COMPLIMENTS
BEAUFORT MEMORIAL HOSPITAL
BEAUFORT COUNTY SCHOOL DISTRICT

Equipped with a list of items that define what their children should be learning, parents evaluate the situation for themselves. Parent–teacher conferences become a dialogue: Parents give and receive information. Parents can expect answers, in specific terms, about how their child is progressing on the standards. Is the teacher teaching what needs to be taught? If not, why not? If so, is their child learning it? If not, what else needs to be done? What can parents do to support their child?

### Involve Parents Early

Don't wait until a child is five years old and on the school doorstep to seek connections with parents. School districts such as **Charlotte-Mecklenburg, NC**, and **Beaufort County, SC**, are starting the school–parent–child connection at birth.

Children do not wait for formal instruction to speak and think. If children do not have a good beginning, they're behind from the start. But nearly 35 percent of the nation's children come to school not fully ready to participate successfully in kindergarten. What happens in the early years is the business of schools, and striking while the iron is hot makes sense.

As Sharon Begley reported in a February 1996 *Newsweek* cover story, experts agree that the learning that takes place in the first five years of children's lives is the most important. If the neurons of infants' and toddlers' brains are stimulated, they become integrated into the brain's circuitry; if the neurons lay idle, they often die.

It's hard to imagine parents who don't want to do right by their children. With a loosely defined contract that identifies the responsibilities of each partner — parents and schools — a child's progress can be monitored closely. Periodic health screenings and a medical referral network support instructional efforts.

➤ Tips for parents, including *How to Get Your Child Ready for School Manual,* a Modern Red Schoolhouse project

**DON'T WAIT UNTIL A CHILD IS FIVE YEARS OLD AND ON THE SCHOOL DOORSTEP TO SEEK CONNECTIONS WITH PARENTS.**

## INVOLVE BUSINESSES IN NEW WAYS

Beyond their important advocacy role, businesses are becoming involved in education in myriad ways that go beyond the traditional donations of old computers and new band uniforms. They're taking the lead in spreading information about the new goals of the system. They're identifying the skills and knowledge workers need. Some are starting to hold students accountable by asking to see grades, portfolios and other progress reports when hiring. In some communities, they're actually helping write new academic content and performance standards; in almost all communities, they're reviewing the standards to make sure they make sense. They're taking charge of mentoring efforts.

For students who do not plan to go directly to college, businesses are helping make the transition from high school to work. Business leaders are helping develop, fund and staff challenging training programs for teachers, superintendents and school boards. They're lending employees to the local school district to teach classes in their area of expertise. And they're giving release time to employees who want to attend conferences and other events at their children's schools.

__Charlotte-Mecklenburg, NC__, Superintendent John Murphy is fond of observing, "Large systems don't change because they see the light. They change because they feel the heat." In many communities, including Charlotte, sustained business pressure has been essential in getting reform started — and in keeping the momentum going.

Political leadership is essential. "Business leaders made it clear that Charlotte needed to build a world-class school system," Murphy says. He adds that his

## IN BEAUFORT

## COMMUNITY INVOLVEMENT YOU CAN SEE

Walk down Bay Street — __Beaufort County, SC's__ five-block main drag — and you see evidence of a community that cares about its schools and its children. In the window of Lipsitz's, a small department store that has been there since the turn of the century, you see a display of student art. Bright, colorful and engaging, it changes with the seasons. Passersby stop to admire and enjoy it.

Across the street and up the block at the Bay Street Trading Company (the local bookstore), the book featured in the window also is attracting a lot of attention. __Downtown Beaufort as a Classroom__ is the work of Lady's Island

middle schoolers, who have done oral histories of old-timers, complete with children's art. The book is simply bound with a spiral binder, but it's eye-catching, selling to tourists as well as Beaufortonians. One teacher says: "The project __Downtown Beaufort as a Classroom__ fits perfectly with my goals for my classroom. It helped strengthen students' basic research skills by using human, written and artifactual (sic) resources."

Walk down __Murfreesboro, TN's__ main street — which is a bit longer than Beaufort's — and stop to have lunch with the superintendent in a restaurant frequented by local business people, folks

from the mayor's office and residents. No sooner are you seated than the chairman of the school board walks in; your host invites him to join you. The meeting is spontaneous and unrehearsed.

Sit down for breakfast in a Beaufort bed and breakfast — the waitress can't serve you fast enough. An old southern custom? Hardly. She has discovered that you're working with the school district. She and her husband (a Marine pilot at the air station) have just been transferred here, and they feel the schools are not rigorous enough. Her child is not working very hard. Tell the superintendent, she says. It's the first thing he hears at our 8 a.m. meeting.

biggest mistake was not keeping business leaders up to date and on the lookout for backsliding. That led to Murphy's eventual resignation.

"I should have paid more attention to the business power structure," he says in retrospect. "I was running the school system and was not keeping the business community informed about the dangers of people undoing what we had done. They got complacent. I got complacent about their complacency. Rather than aggressively support change, they thought they could sit back. Well, the other forces moved back in rapidly. I should have spent more time maintaining positive political support. It can't be the superintendent alone. The community has to take an active role."

> ➤ **Resources on how business is becoming more involved in setting standards**

> ➤ **Resources on how business is using student records when hiring new graduates**

> "LARGE SYSTEMS DON'T CHANGE BECAUSE THEY SEE THE LIGHT. THEY CHANGE BECAUSE THEY FEEL THE HEAT."
>
> — John Murphy

## USE THE MEDIA AND OTHER TOOLS

Public relations and public information are the most poorly understood activities in most school systems. There are two extremes — the "silence is golden" school and the "spin doctor" school.

At one end of the spectrum are unsophisticated districts that fail to communicate with the media or public at all — except when they must, in times of trouble or embarrassment, or when the occasional round of good news crops up. Their theory seems to be *the less said the better.* At the other end of the spectrum are the "sophisticated" districts that carefully get out the story they want told. If they only get the message right, they believe, schools will improve and communities will be happy. Neither approach works to the long-term advantage of the schools. In both cases the public remains ignorant, skeptical and disconnected.

What works is a continuing, active program of open communications with all constituency groups. Involving the press — print and electronic — on a regular basis and establishing regular means of communication among the board, the superintendent, principals and teachers, and the community as a whole are essential. Genuine press involvement should include regular, ongoing meetings with reporters and editorial board members to keep them informed and sympathetic. The more they know about the day-to-day workings of the schools — the ups and downs, the triumphs and the problems — the more faithful and understanding their coverage will be.

At issue here is not a whitewash or "spinning" the news; schools have a complex, multifaceted story to tell, and they should not assume reporters are ready to tell it on their own. Reporters need all the help they can get, including regular on-site meetings with school officials. There is no substitute for first-hand knowledge. Don't wait until your school leads the nation in the production of Merit Scholars to invite the press over for breakfast.

One of the most important things a school district can do to win the goodwill of the press — and improve its own performance — is involve them in one process in particular: the academic analysis. Ask the press what it wants to know about the schools — what kind of data and analyses are important to the press in covering education. If you get them involved at the front end, they're more likely to help you get out the subsequent news about your goals and results.

## IN BEAUFORT

## THE WAGES OF TRUTH

In spring 1994, the **Beaufort County, SC**, schools took a $90 million bond issue to the public and lost by nearly 10 percent of the vote — a shocking vote of no confidence. Instead of hiding in the sand, however, the superintendent and board went forward with vigorous reform efforts — public meetings, standards-setting committees, publications, calls on editorial boards and appearances on every available radio and TV show. They announced plans to return in spring 1995 with a $122 million bond issue, the biggest in the history of South Carolina. Balancing strong board support, a vigorous opposition campaign was fielded, backed by one board member who got ample press coverage. A less-secure board would have turned and run. The Beaufort board didn't. Members convinced the public that they were well on the road to reform, that they were serious and sincere and that with the public's support, they would go the distance. The bond issue passed by a wide margin.

Remember one universal truth: The press is in the habit of covering "breaking news" rather than the more important but less exciting "continuing story." Breaking news is the scandal or disappointment of the moment: arson in the schools, teacher abuse by students, student abuse by teachers, falling test scores, rising test scores, the vote on a bond issue. These stories are legitimate (if not always welcome), but you want them to be told in the context of the larger, continuing story of the schools.

In larger districts the superintendent occasionally may be able to get his or her own TV or radio call-in show — as often as once a month, which is what John Murphy of **Charlotte-Mecklenburg, NC**, did. Most districts have public access TV channels. Go one step beyond airing board meetings; design formats that bring the school to the community. Encourage the local media to cover debate and chess clubs as well as football and basketball teams.

The most important part of media relations is to keep the door open. Schools are the business of the public, and the public has a right to know. Tell the complete story, with candor and confidence. You'll be rewarded for it.

> ➤ **Advice for working with the media, including the** *Guide to Getting Out Your Message* **by the National Education Goals Panel**

**DON'T WAIT UNTIL YOUR SCHOOL LEADS THE NATION IN THE PRODUCTION OF MERIT SCHOLARS TO INVITE THE PRESS OVER FOR BREAKFAST.**

## Beyond the Media

By all means, however, don't rely exclusively on the media to tell your story. In many cases, they are not your most effective communications tool. Research by the Education Commission of the States, for instance, shows that teachers are the most credible source of information for parents and other parents are the next most credible, followed by students. But teachers are kept out of the information loop in most school districts. To help remedy that problem in Philadelphia, a nonprofit group publishes a monthly newsletter for teachers to help the more than 12,000 classroom educators better understand their role in the sweeping reforms under way in their schools and to give them a say in how these changes are being carried out. By giving them practical information to help them in the classroom, the *Philadelphia Teacher* newsletter is providing a tangible benefit to teachers, who in turn are better able to communicate with parents and others.

# STEP 7

TEACHERS
ARE THE MOST
CREDIBLE
SOURCE OF
INFORMATION
FOR PARENTS.

Other districts use a variety of creative techniques to listen to and communicate regularly with parents and other residents; replacing rumors with information in local hairdresser and barber shops — and regularly listening for what other people are saying about the schools — is just one of the tools.

➤ **Resources and tools for going beyond the media to engage the public**

# THERE IS NO
# FINISH LINE

## Making Continuous Improvements

The serious reformer knows that **Step 8** is only last in the sequence, but it is not the last step. Students of organizational behavior know that for vigorous institutions *there is no finish line, only the race.* As former <u>Charlotte-Mecklenburg, NC</u>, Superintendent John Murphy is fond of saying, "Falter and you'll be run over," or in the words of Louis Armstrong, "Once more once."

Successful organizations — whether for-profit, not-for-profit or governmental — do not rest on their laurels. When Xerox restructured, it saved itself, but corporate restructuring is not a one-time process. Effective organizations repeat the process of reinvention but do not cover old ground. The beta sites — each in its own way — have committed themselves to new challenges and opportunities through a process of reinvention and reorientation.

### WHAT'S NEXT?

Step 8, then, is the bridge back to the three basic questions asked at the outset:

* Where are we now?

* Where do we want to be?

* How do we get there?

Asking these questions again and again is essential because their answers depend on context. Each step forward changes the context, as do external factors. Like mountain climbing, as ground is secured, new ground emerges. When the field of vision changes, what one sees changes as well. Consider the steps outlined in this book. Standards are not static, they must be regularly re-examined and upgraded. As standards change, school organization and delivery of instruction must change as well. As teachers, students and administrators become more comfortable with new ways of doing things, still newer ways present themselves. School partnerships need to be tended with care, and new and better ones have to be crafted. Tests and measures must become more sophisticated to reflect new knowledge and new interests. As eternal vigilance is the price of liberty, the battle to deregulate schools is perennial.

## AT A GLANCE

* What's next?

* Secure the beachhead

* Measure yourself against the best

* Continuous improvement

* Institutionalize the revolution

* Maintain public demand for the revolution

SETTING THE
RIGHT PACE IS
THE KEY TO
WINNING A RACE
AND THE KEY
TO REFORMING
SCHOOLS — TOO
FAST AND YOU
BURN OUT (OR
GET RUN OUT OF
TOWN), TOO SLOW
AND THE CRITICS
KILL YOU.

Yesterday's high-performance activity looks quaint today; by the same token, so does yesterday's old-fashioned, input-driven school. Imagine a world-class runner settling for a four-minute mile in the late 1990s; 50 years ago many observers thought the barrier would never be broken. The "streamliner" of the 1950s, the stately ocean liner of the 1930s, the barnstorming biplane of the 1920s, all were wonders when they appeared, but they are reminders of how times and circumstances change.

## SECURE THE BEACHHEAD

Take time to consolidate, to catch your breath, to plan the next steps. Changes in the beta sites have come rapidly, but often incrementally. That is why patience and long-term planning horizons are essential. A frontal assault on old ways is not always as successful as a slower and smoother transition. This is hardly a new insight, but it is one that needs to be constantly relearned.

Setting the right pace is the key to winning a race and the key to reforming schools — too fast and you burn out (or get run out of town), too slow and the critics kill you. How do you find the right pace? Start by choosing the style that best fits your community's circumstances. Play to your strengths.

John Murphy was brought to **Charlotte-Mecklenburg, NC**, to shake up a system, move quickly and not let up the pressure. Says Murphy, "You can change any school in 18 months and make dramatic changes in the whole system within 24 months. Kids spend only six years in elementary school. We have to move quickly to help them."

**Beaufort County, SC**, Superintendent Herman Gaither, a South Carolinian by birth and a product of the local schools who rose to the top, moved decisively and paused now and then for his "troops" to catch up. Unlike Murphy in Charlotte-Mecklenburg, Gaither's roots run deep in the district; he is a reformer who is there to stay. Gaither estimates that Beaufort made 100 major changes in the schools over four years. "Now," he says, "the community is securing the beachhead, making sure the changes have really taken hold, before taking the next major steps. We're going to spend the year talking to our teachers, finding out what's working and what's not, and finding out what assistance they need to be successful."

If you lead a community group, take a page from Beaufort 2000; it worked quietly behind the scenes for a year before going public. If you're a business leader, carefully lay the groundwork for an enterprising superintendent and thoughtful board to forge ahead as they did in **Red Clay, DE**. If you're a board member, do as Bill Manning did in Red Clay: Never relent as long as you hold office.

## MEASURE YOURSELF AGAINST THE BEST

Only by taking stock can an institution improve and continue improving over time. Unhappily, the normal response from many organizations' leaders is to assert that all is well, thank you very much. Saying that is often easy, given the typical points of reference. In affluent Montgomery County, MD, which supposedly has some of the nation's best public schools, the point of reference is typically Washington, DC, with some of the nation's most distressed

### IN BEAUFORT

## COMPETITION WITHIN A DISTRICT? WHAT ABOUT EQUITY?

From technology to site-based budgeting, Herman Gaither, superintendent of the **Beaufort County, SC**, schools, has been clear: Only those principals and schools that demonstrate readiness are given these challenges. Gaither requires each school to earn the right to money or authority and to demonstrate that it can make good financial decisions or put technology to good use. "Make it competitive," he says. "Ask school staff to give you a plan and demonstrate that the school community is ready for the new program, the new materials, the new authority. Allow principals who are ready to join an

elite group. Sibling rivalry occurs in the process. Other principals get with it and come on board the next year. They steal, copy, mimic the high fliers — whatever it takes to make it work. The community adds pressure and sets the expectation: 'If so-and-so has technology, we will have technology in our schools next year.'"

Does this work? In 1992, eight schools got the right to site-based budgeting. Today, all but two of the district's schools have earned the right. Under a competitive system, principals have the ability to self-select and come on

board when they are ready. No one argues about equity — or the lack of it — because the money, authority or program is granted once a school proves it can use it wisely. Gaither's final reflections: "Almost to a person, everyone has stepped up their performance. People who were settling for mediocre have raised the ceiling. People who were lazy have quickly found new energy. The standards have been set. If a principal can't reach them, we help him or her find a gracious way out of the job."

SCHOOLS MUST
DEVELOP THE
HABIT OF
COMPARING
THEMSELVES
TO THE BEST —
ACROSS TOWN,
THROUGHOUT
THE STATE AND
NATION, AND
AROUND THE
GLOBE.

public schools. Evanstown Township north of Chicago does the same. Wellesley, MA, compares itself to Boston and fares quite well by contrast. This habit is so deeply ingrained in American education, we take it for granted.

In sports, the analogy would be the Green Bay Packers comparing themselves to a local high school team rather than to the New England Patriots or the San Francisco 49ers, or the Baltimore Orioles comparing themselves to the Durham Bulls or the Columbus Clippers. Green Bay's local high school team may be terrific, and the Durham Bulls or Columbus Clippers may be fine double A teams. But they are not in the big leagues.

Schools must develop the habit of comparing themselves to the best — across town, throughout the state and nation, and around the globe. Schools should take seriously the **Third International Mathematics and Science Study** (TIMSS) and what it represents. They should use its findings to fine-tune policies and improve practice. And while no individual school can conduct sustained comparative research, schools can support and encourage it through their professional associations, state departments of education and the U.S. Department of Education's Center for Education Statistics.

As a measurement, an academic analysis is not all bad news; it may contain good, even exhilarating news. **Beaufort County, SC**, has learned this lesson. The first round of academic analysis was sobering. Low levels of academic achievement were concentrated among black youngsters throughout the system. But Beaufort's new standards-driven system is helping students' scores climb.

Shifts in attitudes and new technology make it possible for schools to learn from each other in ways hard to imagine a decade ago. Not long ago, our federal system was under attack. Many thought the role of the states had been hopelessly eclipsed by the New Deal. Others thought that too much power was steadily shifting to Washington, DC. Worse yet, the theory ran, the states, left to their own devices, would sink to the lowest common denominator. In terms of academic standards, this decline would mean mindlessness and worse. Not so, as recent experience reveals.

For the first time in memory, states are actively setting standards and are proud of them. **Virginia** was one of the first to be recognized for its high state standards; soon, all 50 states are likely to have standards of their own. And the capacity to compare and contrast them will create pressure for high standards across the nation.

## CONTINUOUS IMPROVEMENT

The gospel of the successful organization is *continuous improvement*. Create a level of performance so high that there are virtually no errors — and continue improving. "Error" rates are not measured as they are in manufacturing, but conceptually the approach is much the same: Senior professionals continuously monitor progress and regularly go back to the drawing board to improve practice.

Standards and school report cards provide improvement examples. One of **Beaufort County, SC's** first steps was to publish a handsome "standards wall chart." Three years into the reform process, parents demanded more detail. The district now has comprehensive, 20-page **standards booklets** available for **K–3 language arts** and **mathematics**. Although the booklets have been received warmly, they are interim documents that will be updated regularly and improved as standards and school performance change. The booklets also serve as a trial balloon for the more complex standards documents that will be developed for upper grades and other subjects over the next few years.

Beaufort's new booklets are as noteworthy for what they do not contain as for what they do. They do not have the names of the superintendent or board on them. The board and superintendent want these documents to faithfully reflect the fact that they are *community* standards.

As for school report cards, Beaufort County, SC, decided that the nomenclature itself was wrong — report cards are for kids, annual reports are for organizations. What might the district's annual reports look like in the

### IN RED CLAY

## PLAGIARISM IS THE SINCEREST FORM OF FLATTERY

**Red Clay, DE**, school officials saw what **Beaufort County, SC**, had done and thought highly of Beaufort's standards wall chart. So they copied it – but Red Clay officials went one better: Not only did they do a standards wall chart, but they also created standards bookmarks, which they pass out in schools and distribute in Wilmington bookstores.

future? As school district and community sophistication increases, the district may produce an electronic report, one that parents, teachers, students, board members, real estate brokers, state legislators — everyone — can read and download from the school district's Web site. Such an annual report could provide depth and breadth, time series data as well as snapshots, text and audio, full-motion and still graphics, testimonials, and communications opportunities. In short, it can be a *virtual school report*, a perfect complement to a visit to the school itself.

## INSTITUTIONALIZE THE REVOLUTION

Maintain momentum, keep up the pace, institutionalize the revolution. The real measure of performance-driven reform is whether the reform outlasts the reformer. Does it have staying power on its own? If reform can only be accomplished and maintained by heroics, if men and women on horseback are central to its success, reform will fail. Management expert Peter Drucker observes that mass education requires ordinary people to do extraordinary things.

Our beta sites provide two major insights: In the first instance, reform is the product of vision, leadership and hard work. People like John Murphy, Herman Gaither, Norman Higgins, John Hodge Jones and Bill Manning make a difference. But every district is endowed with a broad base of talent, energy and capacity. Leadership needs to become the catalyst, releasing and channeling the energy that is already there.

Due to the challenges that are part and parcel of reform, performance-driven schools must be better and more satisfying institutions in which to teach and

## SILENCE CAN BE GOLDEN

The **Beaufort County, SC**, schools' new set of standards describes, in detail, what youngsters need to know and be able to do in the early "grades"; a careful reading of the text shows that these standards are no longer linked to grade levels. District officials are not hiding this transformation, but they are not trumpeting the end of grade levels either. The elimination of grade distinctions is a natural outcome of standards. Age grouping – as distinct from achievement grouping – is an administrative convenience that has outlived its usefulness.

## GORBACHEV'S DILEMMA

Reform-minded superintendents and school boards face what can only be described as Gorbachev's dilemma: To change, centralized systems must be decentralized; the irony is that the decision to decentralize must first be made centrally. Radical decentralization is the *sine qua non* of reform in the modern era, whether it is political reform, business reform or school reform. The top-down, command-control systems of the late 19th and early 20th centuries no longer work. Yet the old command-control organization is still the norm. Short of revolution, how can it be replaced with a modern, democratic form of organization? It takes a strong leader at the center to decentralize: Gorbachev in the Soviet Union; John Murphy in **Charlotte-Mecklenburg, NC**; Herman Gaither in **Beaufort County, SC**; Norman Higgins in **Guilford, ME**; John Hodge Jones in **Murfreesboro, TN**; Bill Manning in **Red Clay, DE**.

learn. They require new incentives and disincentives, new institutional arrangements, a new intellectual infrastructure. The old arrangements must be permanently changed. The new system must become self-regulating, just as the old was. The leader's task is to create a system that can run without him or her.

The secret of accountability is to not dictate. If assistant superintendents and the central office staff are barking orders, they short-circuit the whole process; all members of the organization must be accountable for themselves and their performance. Empower people in the field and the system will run more smoothly and processes will stay in place. The metaphor is the symphony orchestra; there are no great conductors without great musicians. Or as Walt Whitman said, "There can be no great poets without great audiences."

At a more prosaic level, how is this message transmitted? The responses are as varied as the communities from which they spring. With more than 100 schools in **Charlotte-Mecklenburg, NC**, Superintendent John Murphy created a 12-member principal leadership team. Each of the 12 — hand-picked by Murphy — belonged to a network of 11 to 15 schools. The principals worked together collaboratively and met several times between their monthly meetings with Murphy. The principal leadership team gave Murphy access to the experience principals bring to the enterprise. Their message was clear: Focus on academics. Keep the heat on. Encourage local initiative. When

A LEADER NEEDS
TO CREATE AN
ENVIRONMENT
WHERE PEOPLE
FEEL THEY MADE
A DIFFERENCE
AT THE END
OF THE DAY.

— Norm Higgins

something works, spread the good news. When problems appear, worry less about who caused them and more about nipping them in the bud. Murphy's only regret in this regard? "Right from the start, I should have started training my successor to take the reins, someone of a more gentle temperament whose job it would be to maintain the gains when my time was up."

Norm Higgins from **Guilford, ME**, agrees with the importance of training a cadre of leaders. Faculty members from Piscataquis Community High School (where Norm Higgins was principal) assembled a leadership team that includes faculty and the school custodian, who is an alumnus. Higgins says, "Compliance does not build schools; commitment does. Compliance looks good on paper, but it does not get the job done. All the top can do is facilitate change; real change comes from the bottom up. A leader needs to create an environment where people feel they made a difference at the end of the day. How do you do that? For starters, insist on the opportunity to hire new administrators." In small-town Guilford, all key leaders are new: the high school and middle school principals and the elementary supervisor for the five elementary schools. Higgins' words of advice, "Never take a superintendency that you can't walk away from."

**Red Clay, DE**, employs a technique described humorously (if slightly irreverently) as the College of Cardinals. All the principals meet on a weekly basis to provide a sounding board and built-in focus group for the superintendent and other senior staff members. The group does not have formal authority to set or veto policy, but its informal role is considerable. Without the group's buy-in and support, policies (good or bad) won't work. It's a matter of commitment. In his classic, *The English Constitution*, English political analyst Walter Bagehot argues that the absence of a written constitution — which distinguishes the United States from the United Kingdom — does not mean the absence of limits on government.

The medical model suits the school setting: diagnose, prescribe, treat, monitor. Senior professionals monitor progress and regularly go back to the drawing board to improve practice. The other pieces of the medical model fit as well. Doctors aren't wasted as managers. Hospital administrators report to a senior medical team. The profession polices itself because it has the knowledge and will to do so. The analogy in the district is a standing committee of senior staff members, teachers and citizens to monitor school performance and oversee the process of course correction and improvement. Site-managed schools where faculty control their own budgets and don't have to go looking for funds push decision-making even farther down the ranks.

## MAINTAIN PUBLIC DEMAND FOR THE REVOLUTION

Finally, ignore your community at your own risk. John Murphy's commentary on the text of school reform centers on **Charlotte-Mecklenburg, NC's** business community, which had been forceful in the beginning, but gradually lost its focus and energy about the schools. Executives were distracted by day-to-day business and the excitement of participating in Charlotte's growth. Murphy admits he was part of the problem. He did not continue to cultivate business leaders as ardently as he had in the beginning. At the end of the third year, a major bond issue failed for lack of support. Its centerpiece was a technical high school for downtown Charlotte. Offered an old department store, Murphy had proposed a high school of banking and the arts (including culinary arts, with a student-run restaurant and catering service). For the nation's fourth largest banking center, the idea was a natural. Yet the bond issue failed by a handful of votes. The business community did not bear down as it had for

## IN BEAUFORT

## WATCH YOUR GARDEN GROW

In addition to a deep commitment to high academic standards, **Beaufort County, SC**, Superintendent Herman Gaither is a gifted communicator — precise, forceful and eloquent. His presentations are organized as well as convincing, in the best traditions of classic Southern oratory. Gaither's talent for communicating extends to teachers, students and the public. After Beaufort's first bond issue failed in 1994, he stumped the district for weeks on the second; it passed by a wide margin. Gaither believes the school reform story is not a matter of spin but a matter of telling the truth, fully and regularly. The community can tolerate bad news, but it will not countenance lies or half truths, or equally as bad, no news.

Awed both by the amount of energy Gaither dedicates to the public and the obvious payoffs, both Murphy (formerly of **Charlotte-Mecklenburg, NC**) and Jones (of **Murfreesboro, TN**) express newfound respect for the power of keeping the community fires stoked. As Jones noted about his action to extend the day in Murfreesboro, "The road to this deceptively simple reform was, to say the least, rocky. My biggest surprise was convincing the community that it made sense to change. I made the change first, then went out to sell it. I was hopelessly naive about the difficulties I would face. I intend to call Superintendent Gaither about how I can do things differently in the future. I want to know what he knows."

## LET A THOUSAND FLOWERS BLOOM: A VAST ARRAY OF RESOURCES

The alert reader will have noted that we have scrupulously avoided endorsing any single or even multiple sets of standards or groups of standards setters. Indeed, the essence of the process we recommend is local adoption of locally created standards and assessments. But this does not mean that everything must be reinvented, or that there is no standards work going on in other places that is not useful. To the contrary, other standards-setting activities are invaluable, and their numbers are growing. The more the merrier. Our only caveat is that you do some hard, independent thinking before you turn to others.

Having said this, we highlight a few that are known to us, including ACHIEVE, American Federation of Teachers, Council for Basic Education, Education Trust, Florida Chamber of Commerce Foundation, New American Schools, National Board for Professional Teaching Standards, National Center on Education and the Economy and National Alliance of Business, and urge you to look at what they are doing. Your time will not be wasted. We also invite those of you online to enlarge this book, both for our benefit and the benefit of school reformers wherever they may be. Contact information for these organizations is on page 169.

➤ **Organizations that can guide standards-setting efforts**

the new professional basketball team. Murphy resigned six months after the bond vote. As important as bond issues are, Murphy believes the most vital role the business community can play is to provide a cadre of highly qualified candidates for the school board by nominating and electing people who care about education but have a business-like approach to their responsibilities. Murphy ruefully admits that he should have tended the business garden more faithfully.

---

This book attempts to distill the vision of performance-driven schools, tell the story in simple English and provide interested reformers with success stories as well as practical guidance. *Raising the Standard's* purpose is to provide the facts and build confidence. The beta sites are doing it. You can do it. Reform is not fanciful, not a quixotic dream, but within reach of any community willing to commit itself. That, in the final analysis, is the lesson of the beta sites. If they can reform their schools, any community in America can.

# HAVE YOU DONE THIS?
## CHECKLIST

## A Checklist of Action Steps

**Step 1**
Take the Plunge: Building Public Demand
For Standards and Reform

Have you:
- ✔ Taken the pulse of your community?
- ✔ Reframed the issues?
- ✔ Built capacity for sustained improvement?

**Step 2**
How Good Is Good Enough? Organizing
Around High Academic Standards

Have you:
- ✔ Developed academic content standards?
- ✔ Used the right criteria for a good standard?
- ✔ Built community consensus?
- ✔ Overhauled the curriculum?

**Step 3**
The Truth Will Set You Free: Conducting
An Academic Analysis

Have you:
- ✔ Decided to conduct an academic analysis?
- ✔ Pulled the data together and then pulled it apart?
- ✔ Used the data to inform and make decisions to improve learning?

**Step 4**
Seize the Day: Reorganizing for Change
And Building Staff Capacity

Have you:
- ✔ Focused on results, not rules?
- ✔ Given principals and teachers more control?
- ✔ Changed the orientation of the central office?
- ✔ Tailored instruction to students?
- ✔ Used time differently?
- ✔ Rethought teacher development?
- ✔ Given principals new leadership and management skills?

**Step 5**
Measuring Up: Holding Students
Accountable

Have you:
- ✔ Developed better tests?
- ✔ Used a mix of tests?
- ✔ Involved teachers?
- ✔ Given people time to adjust?

**Step 6**
Holding Your Feet to the Fire: School
And District Accountability

Have you:
- ✔ Set challenging goals?
- ✔ Evaluated principals?
- ✔ Evaluated teachers?
- ✔ Evaluated your superintendent?
- ✔ Assessed customer satisfaction?
- ✔ Publicized goals and results?

**Step 7**
So What's in It for Me? Developing
New Partnerships

Have you:
- ✔ Challenged your community?
- ✔ Involved the community in new ways?
- ✔ Involved parents in new ways?
- ✔ Involved businesses in new ways?
- ✔ Used the media and other tools?

**Step 8**
There Is No Finish Line: Making
Continuous Improvements

Have you:
- ✔ Secured the beachhead?
- ✔ Measured yourself against the best?
- ✔ Continued to improve?
- ✔ Institutionalized the revolution?
- ✔ Maintained public demand for the revolution?

# ABOUT THE
# AUTHORS

**Denis Philip Doyle**, founder of Doyle Associates, is a nationally and internationally known education writer, lecturer and consultant. After earning his bachelor of arts degree ('62) and master of arts degree ('64) in political theory from the University of California at Berkeley, he worked for the California state legislature, where he was the architect of major education bills, including the Ryan Act. He became assistant director of the U.S. Office of Economic Opportunity in 1972, then assistant director of the National Institute of Education. He has been associated with "think tanks" since 1980 — Brookings, American Enterprise Institute, Heritage and Hudson Institute, where he is presently a senior fellow. He has written numerous scholarly and popular articles for publications including *The Atlantic, The Public Interest, Change, Education Week* and the *Phi Delta Kappan* and published more than 150 op-eds in the nation's most prestigious newspapers: *The Washington Post, The Wall Street Journal, The Los Angeles Times,* and the *Baltimore Sun.* Three of his books in print are ***Investing in Our Children: Business and the Public Schools*** (CED, New York, NY, 1984), ***Winning the Brain Race: A Bold Plan to Make Our Schools Competitive*** (with David T. Kearns, Xerox CEO, 1989 and 1991) and ***Reinventing Education: Entrepreneurship in America's Public Schools*** (with Louis V. Gerstner, IBM CEO, et al., 1994). With underwriting from Rockwell International, he wrote a year-long series of "advertorials" about education for *The Atlantic* and wrote "Children of Promise" for *Business Week.* He was appointed by U.S. Secretary of Education Lamar Alexander to the National Education Commission on Time and Learning. He lectures on education change at home and abroad. He is married to Gloria Revilla and is the father of two children, Alicia and Christopher. He lives and works in Chevy Chase, MD.

**Susan Pimentel** specializes in standards-driven school reform and works as an education writer, analyst and consultant. After earning a bachelor of science in early childhood education and a law degree from Cornell University, Pimentel worked in the Maryland state legislature. She served as senior policy advisor for Gov. William Donald Schaefer and then as special counsel to former Superintendent John Murphy in Prince George's County, MD, the nation's 16th largest school district. Her efforts resulted in the phase-out of student tracking, an enriched core curricula, advances in school-site management and a results-based school accountability program. Subsequently, she was director of the World Class Schools Panel (impaneled to sculpt a concrete plan of action for school transformation) in Charlotte-

Mecklenburg, NC. In recent years, her work has focused on academic standards with corresponding work in principal evaluation, student assessment and school accountability. Her efforts stress standards-setting, constituency-building, policy analysis and strategic planning in such varied jurisdictions as Beaufort County, SC; Chicago, IL; Jackson, TN; Red Clay, DE; and the states of Arizona and Pennsylvania. The method to transform schools outlined in this book combines "process" and "substance" to develop communities and organize around standards. The process is democratic with a small "d" — involving teachers, principals, parents, community leaders and students in structured teams. The substance is high and rigorous standards comparable to those of our competitors abroad. Pimentel currently is serving as senior standards advisor to the California Academic Standards Commission. The first two content area drafts in language arts and mathematics have drawn national praise. Her most recent article, "Grading Principals: Administrator Evaluations Come of Age," with John Murphy, describes a results-based evaluation and profit-sharing system. Pimentel lives in Hanover, NH, with her daughter, Yardley.

# ADVISORY
# COMMITTEE

Jeanne Allen, President
Center for Education Reform
Washington, DC

Bruce Cooper
Fordham University/Coopers & Lybrand
New York City, NY

Howard Fuller, Director
Institute for the Transformation of Learning
Marquette University
Milwaukee, WI

Herman Gaither, Superintendent
Beaufort County Schools
Beaufort County, SC

Norman Higgins, Superintendent
Guilford School District
Guilford, ME

John Hodge Jones, Superintendent
Murfreesboro City Schools
Murfreesboro, TN

Bill Manning, President
Red Clay Board of Education
Wilmington, DE

John Murphy
ARVIDA Company
Boca Raton, FL

Adam Urbanski, President
Rochester Teachers Association
Rochester, NY

# CONTACT INFORMATION

## Organizations That Can Guide Standards-Setting Efforts

**ACHIEVE**
1280 Massachusetts Ave., Suite 410
Cambridge, MA 02138
617-496-6300
fax: 617-496-6361
www.achieve.org
Contact: Robert Schwartz, President

**American Federation of Teachers**
555 New Jersey Ave., NW
Washington, DC 20001
202-879-4400
fax: 202-393-6371
www.aft.org
Contact: Heidi Glidden, 202-393-7476

**Council for Basic Education**
1319 F St., NW, Suite 900
Washington, DC 20004-1152
202-347-4171
fax: 202-347-5047
Contact: Selina Newell Winchester
e-mail: info@c-b-e.org

**The Education Trust**
1725 K St., NW, Suite 200
Washington, DC 20006
202-293-1217
fax: 202-293-2605
www.edtrust.org
Contact: Patte Barth
e-mail: pbarth@edtrust.org

**Florida Chamber of Commerce**
136 South Bronough St.
P.O. Box 11309
Tallahassee, FL 32302
904-425-1200
fax: 904-425-1260
http://worldclass.flchamb.com
Contact: Jane D. McNabb, Executive Vice
President
e-mail: jmcnabb@flachamb.com

**Leadership Learning Systems**
406 East Main St.
Yorkville, IL 60560
708-553-1727
Contact: Gail Digate, President

**National Alliance of Business**
Business Coalition for Education Reform
1201 New York Ave., NW, Suite 700
Washington, DC 20005
202-289-2888
fax: 202-289-1303
www.nab.com
www.bcer.org
Contact: Aimee R. Guidera, 202-289-2901
e-mail: guidera@nab.com

**National Board for Professional Teaching
Standards**
26555 Evergreen Rd., Suite 400
Southfield, MI 48076
800-229-9074
fax: 248-351-4170
www.nbpts.org
Contact: James A. Kelly, President

**National Center on Education and the Economy**
700 11th St., NW, Suite 750
Washington, DC 20001
202-783-3668
fax: 202-783-3672
www.ncee.org
Contact: Mary Anne Mays
e-mail: mmays@ncee.org

**National Education Association**
1201 16th St., NW
Washington, DC 20036
202-822-7200
fax: 202-822-7292
www.nea.org
Contact: Communications Department

**New American Schools**
1000 Wilson Blvd., Suite 2710
Arlington, VA 22209
703-908-9500
fax: 703-908-0622
www.naschools.org
Contact: Mary Anne Schmitt, 703-908-0625
e-mail: info@nasdc.org

# EXPLORE THE CD-ROM

## Index for the CD-ROM Appendix

Explore the CD-ROM version of *Raising the Standard* for more detailed information on these topics:

### ACCOUNTABILITY

### ASSESSMENTS

### BEAUFORT COUNTY, SC

## MURFREESBORO, TN

## RED CLAY, DE

## RESOURCES

Tips for parents, including *How to Get Your Child Ready for School Manual*, a Modern Red Schoolhouse project *pg. 147*

## STANDARDS